INDIA AND SAARC ENGAGEMENTS

INDIA AND SAARC ENGAGEMENTS

(In 2 Volumes)

(Volume-2)

Editor
Dr. O.P. Goel

ISHA BOOKS
DELHI-110 033

India and SAARC Engagements

ISBN: 81-8205-120-7 (Set)
ISBN: 81-8205-121-5 (Vol. 1)

Published in 2004 in India by
Isha Books, D-43, Prithviraj Road,
Adarsh Nagar, Delhi-110 033

Laser Typesetting at : Shree Vaishnavi Creations, Delhi
Printed at : Chawla Offset Press, Delhi

Contents

International Political Developments; Dates and Venue of the Eleventh Meeting of the Heads of State or Government.

Preface

The South Asian Association for Regional Cooperation (SAARC) comprises the seven countries of South Asia, i.e. Bangladesh, Bhutan, India, the Maldives, Nepal, Pakistan and Sri Lanka. It is an association based on the consciousness that in an increasingly interdependent world, the objectives of peace, freedom, social justice and economic prosperity are best achieved in the South Asian region by fostering mutual understanding, good neighbourly relations and meaningful cooperation among the member states which are bound by ties of history and culture.

The present publication is an attempt to understand the Indian policy perspective in South Asia in a larger context of the phenomenon of regional integration across the world. Within the subcontinent, India's national security interests are closely linked to her immediate neighbours namely Myanmar, Bangladesh, Bhutan, Nepal, Sri Lanka, Maldives and Pakistan. Her relations with Nepal, Bhutan, Bangladesh, Sri Lanka and Maldives are basically stable. However, there is potential for further reinforcing the relationship both in the SAARC framework and at bilateral levels.

Role of SAARC in the development of South Asia (India in particular) is elaboratively described in this book. Details of SAARC summits and regional conventions are also discribed. It also outlines the Indian policy and approach to regionalism in South Asia in the historical context of foreign policy ideas and ideology formulated by the Indian leadership before and after India's independence and emergence as a modern nation state.

Editor

1

History and Evolution of SAARC

The South Asian Association for Regional Cooperation (SAARC) comprises the seven countries of South Asia, i.e. Bangladesh, Bhutan, India, the Maldives, Nepal, Pakistan and Sri Lanka. It is an Association based on the consciousness that in an increasingly interdependent world, the objectives of peace, freedom, social justice and economic prosperity are best achieved in the South Asian region by fostering mutual understanding, good neighbourly relations and meaningful cooperation among the Member States which are bound by ties of history and culture.

The idea of regional cooperation in South Asia was first mooted in May 1980. After consultations, the Foreign Secretaries of the seven countries met for the first time in Colombo in April 1981. This was followed by a meeting of the Committee of the Whole in Colombo in August-September 1981, which identified five broad areas for regional cooperation.

The Foreign Ministers of South Asia, at their first meeting in New Delhi in August 1983, adopted the

Declaration on South Asian Regional Cooperation (SARC) and formally launched the Integrated Programme of Action (IPA) initially in five agreed areas of cooperation namely, Agriculture; Rural Development; Telecommunications; Meteorology; and Health and Population Activities.

The Heads of State or Government at their First SAARC Summit held in Dhaka on 7-8 December 1985 adopted the Charter formally establishing the South Asian Association for Regional Cooperation (SAARC).

The objectives, principles and general provisions contained in the SAARC Charter are as follows:

Objectives

- To promote the welfare of the peoples of South Asia and to improve their quality of life;
- To accelerate economic growth, social progress and cultural development in the region and to provide all individuals the opportunity to live in dignity and to realise their full potential;
- To promote and strengthen collective self-reliance among the countries of South Asia;
- To contribute to mutual trust, understanding and appreciation of one another's problems;
- To promote active collaboration and mutual assistance in the economic, social, cultural, technical and scientific fields;
- To strengthen cooperation with other developing countries;

— To strengthen cooperation among themselves in international forums on matters of common interests; and

— To cooperate with international and regional organisations with similar aims and purposes.

Principles

— Cooperation within the framework of the Association is based on respect for the principles of sovereign equality, territorial integrity, political independence, noninterference in the internal affairs of other States and mutual benefit;

— Such cooperation is to complement and not to substitute bilateral or multilateral cooperation; and

— Such cooperation should be consistent with bilateral and multilateral obligations of Member States.

General Provisions

— Decisions at all levels in SAARC are to be taken on the basis of unanimity; and

— Bilateral and contentious issues are to be excluded from the deliberations of the Association.

Institutional Setup

The Charter of the Association provides for the following:

The Summit

The highest authority of the Association rests with the Heads of State or Government, who meet annually at the Summit level. To date, eleven Summits have been held: Dhaka (1985), Bangalore (1986), Kathmandu (1987), Islamabad (1988), Malé (1990), Colombo (1991), Dhaka (1993), New Delhi (1995), Malé (1997), Colombo (1998) and Kathmandu (2002). The Twelfth SAARC Summit is scheduled to be held in Pakistan.

The Council of Ministers

Comprising the Foreign Ministers of Member States, the Council is responsible for formulating policies; reviewing progress; deciding on new areas of cooperation; establishing additional mechanisms as deemed necessary; and deciding on other matters of general interest to the Association.

The Council is expected to meet twice a year and may also meet in extraordinary sessions by agreement of Member States. It has held twenty-three regular sessions.

To mark the First Decade of SAARC, a Commemorative Session of the Council was held in New Delhi on 18 December 1995 during the Sixteenth Session of the Council of Ministers. Informal meetings of the Council are also held on the sidelines of the United Nations General Assembly Sessions in New York.

The Standing Committee

The Standing Committee comprising the Foreign Secretaries of Member States is entrusted with the task of overall monitoring and coordination of programmes; approving of projects and programmes, and modalities of financing; determining inter-sectoral priorities; mobilising regional and external resources; and identifying new areas of cooperation. It meets as often as deemed necessary and submits its reports to the Council of Ministers.

The Committee has held Twenty-eight regular sessions and three special sessions. The Fourth Special Session of the Standing Committee being held in Kathmandu on 9-10 July 2003.

The Standing Committee is authorised to set up Action Committees comprising Member States concerned with implementation of projects involving more than two but less than seven Member States.

The Standing Committee is assisted by a Programming Committee (which is not a SAARC Charter body) comprising senior officials to scrutinize the Secretariat Budget, finalise the Calendar of Activities and take up any other matter assigned to it by the Standing Committee. The Programming Committee has also been entrusted to consider and submit to the Standing Committee recommendations for action on the Reports of the Technical Committees, SAARC Regional Centres and the SAARC Audio Visual Exchange (SAVE) Committee. The Programming Committee has held twentythree sessions.

The Technical Committees

At present, there are seven Technical Committees functioning in various fields under the agreed areas of cooperation. The Technical Committees formulate specialized programmes and projects in their respective fields under the SAARC Integrated Programme of Action (SIPA).

They are also responsible for monitoring the implementation of such activities and submit their reports to the Standing Committee through the Programming Committee.

Six meetings of planners have been held so far, i.e. one in 1983 and five annually from 1987 to 1991. These meetings initiated cooperation in important areas such as trade, manufactures and services; basic needs; human resources development; database on socio-economic indicators; energy modeling techniques; plan modeling techniques; and poverty alleviation strategies.

Specialised Ministerial Meetings

Since the establishment of the Association, a number of SAARC ministerial meetings have been held to focus attention on specific areas of common concern, and these have now become an integral part of the consultative structure.

The following ministerial-level meetings have been held so far:

— International Economic issues - Islamabad (1986)

— Children - New Delhi (1986), Colombo (1992) and Rawalpindi (1996)

— Women's issues - Shillong (1986), Islamabad (1990), Kathmandu (1993) and Dhaka (1995)

— Environment - New Delhi (1992 & 1997), Malé (1997), Colombo (1998) and Thimphu (2002)

— Disabled Persons - Islamabad (1993)

— Youth - Malé (1994)

— Poverty Alleviation - Dhaka (1994), New Delhi (1996) and Islamabad (2002)

— Housing - Colombo (1996)

— Agriculture - Islamabad (1996) and Kathmandu (2002)

— Trade - New Delhi (1996), Islamabad (1998), Dhaka (1999), Malé (1999) and New Delhi (2001)

— Tourism - Colombo (1997)

— Information - Dhaka (1998) and Islamabad (2002)

— Communications - Colombo (1998)

— Culture – Colombo (2003)

An emergency meeting of SAARC Health Ministers was convened in Male' on 29 April 2003 on the subject of Severe Acute Respiratory Syndrome (SARS). This was the first time in which SAARC Ministers have met to hold consultations in short notice to evolve a common strategy for tackling an emerging urgent issue.

The SAARC Integrated Programme of Action (SIPA)

At the time SAARC was established in 1985, the core of its work programme was the Integrated Programme of Action (IPA) consisting of a number of Technical Committees on agreed areas of cooperation. However, as the agreed Agenda of SAARC expanded, new areas were identified for regional cooperation. The IPA too expanded correspondingly. Given the emphasis laid down at successive Summits on the need to consolidate and streamline the IPA and make it more result oriented, a set of guidelines and procedures was adopted in 1992 for rationalisation of SAARC activities. The objective was to focus more on activities that would yield The Standing Committee in 1996 reviewed the institutional mechanisms and activities of the Association. This included an evaluation of the mandate and functions of the Technical Committees as well as the role of the Secretariat.

An Independent Group of Experts set up by the Secretary-General in 1997 also undertook an extensive review of the functioning of the IPA and made wide-ranging recommendations. These were considered by the Standing Committee at its Twenty-sixth Session held in Nuwara Eliya, Sri Lanka in March 1999. It proposed a newly restructured SAARC Integrated Programme of Action (SIPA), which was approved by the Council of Ministers at its Twenty-first Session.

Under the reconstituted SIPA, the number of Technical Committees has been reduced from eleven to seven mainly through the amalgamation of different areas covered by the erstwhile Technical Committees thereby eliminating overlapping and duplication. The prime objective of the reorganisation has been to enhance clarity in terms of goals and targets of the activities as well as to improve their quality and efficacy.

The seven Technical Committees under SIPA now cover:

1. Agriculture and Rural Development;
2. Communications and Transport;

3. Social Development;
4. Environment, Meteorology and Forestry;
5. Science and Technology;
6. Human Resources Development; and
7. Energy.

An in-built mechanism for automatic review of activities under SIPA has been provided for. The review will be undertaken every three years by an independent multidisciplinary Expert Group to be constituted by the Secretary-General in consultation with Member States. Accordingly, an Inter-Governmental Committee set up to review the functioning of SIPA met at the SAARC Secretariat on 2-3 November 2002 and made a number of recommendations.

The Fourth Special Session of the Standing Committee is expected to examine the recommendations of the Inter-Governmental Committee on the subject. The Secretary-General is authorised to propose activities and programmes under SIPA and to make specific recommendations to the Standing Committee regarding the mobilisation of necessary resources for the approved activities. This enables the Secretary-General to explore funding possibilities for specific activities from within the region and other acceptable sources.

The Secretary-General reports to the Standing Committee on the progress of the implementation of the SIPA both at its inter-Summit and pre-Summit sessions. The areas of work assigned to respective Technical Committees are as follows:

Technical Committee on Agriculture and Rural Development

As per the reconstituted SIPA, the two Technical Committees on Agriculture and Rural Development were merged into one as the Technical Committee on Agriculture and Rural Development. The reconstituted Committee under the chairmanship of Nepal started functioning in 2000 and has since held two meetings.

During its Second Meeting, the Committee reviewed the progress since its First Meeting. It discussed the common SAARC position for a regional strategy on the World Food Summit: five years later (10-13 June 2002, Rome). Nepal, being the present Chair of SAARC, briefed the Meeting about the common SAARC position which was placed before the Summit. The Committee also reviewed its activities and those financed by the SAARC-Japan Special Fund during the year 2001/2002. It discussed the two theme papers namely (a) Enhancing Food Production through storage, processing and quality control, including aspects of distribution, and (b) Role of Local Authorities in Rural Employment and Poverty Alleviation through the enhancement of agricultural output.

The Meeting decided that the theme for the next meeting would be "Water Resources Management for Agriculture in SAARC Countries." It discussed the draft Terms of Reference (TOR) on establishing a "SAARC Quadrangle Milk Grid" prepared by Nepal. The Meeting requested Nepal to revise the Concept Paper on "Exchange of Rural Development Volunteers in the SAARC Countries."

The calendar of activities for the year 2003-2004 includes:

Workshop on Food Security (Pakistan); Seminar on Improvement of Quality of Livestock and Fisheries Products (Pakistan); Workshop on Role of Local Authorities in Rural Employment and Poverty Alleviation (Bangladesh); and Workshop on Harmonization of Standards on Food Products (Nepal).

Technical Committee on Communications and Transport

Following the decision taken at the Twenty-sixth Session of the Standing Committee (Nuwara Eliya, March 1999), the Technical Committee on Communications and Transport has been entrusted with the work of the two erstwhile Technical Committees on Telecommunications and on Transport. In addition, broader issues relating to telecommunications and postal services are also being addressed by the Committee. The Technical Committee on Communications and Transport has held two meetings on 5-6 January 2001 and 12-14 September 2002 respectively. Both the meetings were held under the chairmanship of Pakistan. During its second meeting, the Committee reviewed the progress in implementation of the Plan of Action on Telecommunications adopted by the First SAARC Communications Ministers' Conference in 1998. While doing so, it recommended that due to fast and innovative developments in the field of telecommunications, the Plan of Action would need to be revised.

As regards evolving a common position at the World Summit on Information Society (WSIS) in Geneva in December 2003, issues pertaining to the telecom sector were identified by the Committee for consideration by the next Communications Ministers' Conference. In Postal Services sector, the Committee deliberated on various issues including the Study on Postal Transit Facilities in Member Countries; Letter Writing Competitions that are held annually; and the proposal to issue special commemorative stamps to coincide with the SAARC Charter Day (8 December).

The Committee also discussed issues related to Transport sector including a Compendia of Information on Roads; a Study on Transport Infrastructure and Transit Facilities in the region; Highway Safety; and Public Passenger Transport. The activities proposed for 2003 include: Transport Project Planning Course (Pakistan); Workshop on enforcement of traffic laws (Bangladesh); Workshop on urban transportation system (Bangladesh); Seminar on road slope stabilization (Nepal); Eighteenth Letter Writing Competition (Nepal); Seminar on highway safety (Pakistan); Workshop on quality management and customer care in postal system (Pakistan); and Workshop on cellular telephony (Pakistan).

Technical Committee on Social Development

Under the reconstituted SIPA, the Technical Committee on Social Development subsumes the work of the two erstwhile Technical Committees, namely Health, Population Activities and Child Welfare, and Women in Development. In addition, broader issues relating to drug de-addiction, rehabilitation of drug addicts and demand reduction are also addressed by the Social Development Committee.

The Committee held its first meeting in March 2002 in Kathmandu under the chairmanship of Maldives. During its meeting, the Committee considered the decisions/directives of the Eleventh Summit in the social sector with regard to inter-alia: (a) Convention on Regional Arrangements for the Promotion of Child Welfare in South Asia, (b) Convention on Preventing and Combating Trafficking in Women and Children for Prostitution, (c) formation of an Autonomous Advocacy Group of Prominent Women Personalities, and (d) formation of a Task Force to review status of implementation of past decisions in the social sector and to suggest guidelines for their effective implementation.

Technical Committee on Environment, Meteorology and Forestry

Environment has remained as an important agenda in the SAARC process since 1987. Under the reconstituted SIPA, the Technical Committee on Environment and that on Meteorology were merged into a single Technical Committee on Environment and Meteorology. This Committee was also charged with the additional subject of Forestry and has since held two meetings in 2001 and 2002 under the chairmanship of Bhutan.

Earlier, the Technical Committee on Meteorology initiated the practice of awarding annual Regional Awards to young scientists or a group of scientists for their contributions in the field of meteorology. Another award has also been introduced since 1995 to senior scientists. This practice has been continuing even after the merger of Meteorology into the Technical Committee on Environment, Meteorology and Forestry.

The Second Meeting of the Committee, which was held in Thimphu in August 2002, reviewed the status of implementation of the decisions taken at its First Meeting as well as those of the Fourth SAARC Environment Ministers' Conference. This included the Colombo Declaration for a Common Environment Programme adopted in 1998 for which the Committee recommended focusing on a single theme in each of the future meetings, with a view to identifying specific environmental projects within the region. The Committee also deliberated on the presentation of a common SAARC position at the World Summit for Sustainable Development (Johannesburg, 27 August – 4 September 2002). The Committee further discussed the status of implementation of the Plan of Action on Environment which called for preparation of National Stateof-the-Environment reports; circulation of the latest National Action Plan on Environment; provision of a list of national forestry institutions; holding of a Workshop on Climate Change; and consideration of a Regional Treaty on Environment.

The calendar of activities for the year 2002-2003 includes:

Seminar on Transport and Related Environment Issues (Bangladesh); Workshop on Solid Waste Management (Bangladesh); Seminar on Climatic Data Management (Sri Lanka); Meeting of Experts to Strengthen Environment Management Infrastructure (India); Meeting of Experts from SAARC Countries to evolve a common approach for access to genetic resources (Sri Lanka); Expert Group Meeting on Bio-safety to consider establishing a cooperative framework for the exchange of genetic resources and associated traditional knowledge to safeguard the interests of the region's bio-diversity (SAARC Secretariat, Kathmandu); and Expert Group Meeting to consider the pre-feasibility study of setting up the SAARC Coastal Zone Management Centre (Maldives).

Technical Committee on Science and Technology The Technical Committee on Science and Technology came into being in 1983. Since then, the Committee has formulated and implemented a variety of regional programmes including organization of expert group meetings, seminars, workshops and training programmes, and preparation of state-of-the-art reports and directories on various subjects with a view to developing the scientific and technological skills in Member States through increased cooperation. Ever since its establishment, the Committee has held sixteen meetings under the erstwhile IPA.

Under the reconstituted SAARC Integrated Programme of Action (SIPA), the Committee has held two meetings under the chairmanship of India. The Second Meeting of the Technical Committee on Science and Technology, after reviewing progress, gave special emphasis on Biotechnology and discussed its present state, and ways and means to improve it. The Committee reviewed progress in the field of Science and Technology, e.g. SAARC Technology Initiative, Cooperation in Biotechnology, Technology Transfer and New Areas in Biotechnology. The calendar of activities for 2003 includes: Biosafety and Bioethics Priorities (Bangladesh);

Training Course on the Use of GPS Technology in Hazard Assessment and GPS Data Processing (India); Biosafety Issues in the Use of Recombinant Technologies (India); Symposium on Natural Product Chemistry (Pakistan); and Training Course on Bio-assays and

Pharmacological Techniques for Drug Development (Pakistan).

Technical Committee on Human Resources Development

The first meeting of the Technical Committee on Human Resources Development under the restructured SIPA took place in Colombo on 18-20 October 2001. The meeting discussed the scope of the Committee and decided that the following areas specific to its mandate as per the decision of the Twenty-sixth Session of the Standing Committee would guide the future work of the Committee: (a) education; (b) culture; (c) sports; and (d) youth development. During its second meeting in Colombo on 7-8 November 2002, emphasis was given on strengthening cooperation in human resources development among Member Countries. It decided to establish a network of nodal agencies dealing with the subject in all Member Countries for close coordination as well as sharing experiences.

The Committee deliberated on a wide range of issues for strengthening cooperation among Member Countries including education, culture, sports and youth development. It also revised the SAARC Chairs, Fellowships and Scholarships Scheme and recommended it for approval by higher SAARC bodies. The meeting recommended eight activities in the areas of education, culture, sports and youth development for the year 2003. These are: Training of Coaches for Squash (Pakistan); Writers and Publishers Forum (India); Seventh Archaeological Congress (India); SAARC Cultural Festival (Bangladesh); Workshop/Seminar on Youth Employment Generation Strategies in the SAARC

Countries (Bhutan); Training Programme for Physical Educational Trainers and Coaches (India); Workshop on the role of vocational and technical education in poverty alleviation in SAARC Countries (Nepal); and Workshop on Capacity Building of Supervisory Staff of Rural Schools (Sri Lanka).

Technical Committee on Energy

Cooperation in the energy sector was brought under the purview of the SAARC Integrated Programme of Action (SIPA) in January 2000 by establishing a new Technical Committee on Energy.

The objectives of the Technical Committee are to develop a common understanding on energy cooperation in South Asia; to provide a forum for discussion on ways and means of developing and harnessing the existing energy resources within the region; to facilitate exchange of information between Governments, the private sector, and experts and appropriate community-based organizations active in the field; to consider modalities/ technical details regarding establishment of an appropriate South Asian Energy Grid; and to consider the desirability and feasibility of obtaining supplementary technical and other resources from regional and international partners.

The First Meeting of the Technical Committee on Energy was held in Dhaka on 17-18 November 2002 under the chairmanship of Bangladesh. The Meeting emphasized on the importance of use of environment-friendly energy sources. While natural gas has been treated as environment friendly, some of the delegations felt that hydro-electricity and other renewable energy are also environment friendly and should be taken into consideration. It recommended that an institutional framework be established with the initiative from SAARC Secretariat for sharing experiences and information on energy. Such a framework is meant to provide a basis for exchanging expertise, experiences and information on success stories of the Member Countries to facilitate regional or country level programmes on energy. The Meeting also recommended sharing of experience in the field of rural electrification and participation of private sector in supporting initiatives in energy.

Regional Centres

The five regional centres established in Member Countries promote regional cooperation in different areas assigned to them. Each Centre is managed by a Governing Board. The Board comprises representatives of Member States, SAARC Secretary-General and the Ministry of Foreign/External Affairs of the host government. The Director of the Centre acts as Member Secretary to the Governing Board which reports to the Standing Committee.

The Third Special Session of the Standing Committee (Colombo, August 2001) entrusted the Secretary-General to undertake a performance audit of all the Regional Centres in order to take stock of their practical outputs with regard to regional cooperation, to evaluate their mandates and to suggest ways and means of improving their functioning.

Accordingly, the Secretary-General undertook the performance audit of all the Centres. Pursuant to a decision of the Twenty-seventh Session of the Standing Committee (Kathmandu, January 2002), a meeting of the Group of Experts from Member States was held at the SAARC Secretariat in May 2002 to review financial and administrative regulations of the SAARC Regional Centres as well as to consider the recommendations of the Secretary-General on the performance audit of the Centres. The Twenty-eighth Session of the Standing Committee endorsed the above recommendations.

SAARC Agricultural Information Centre (SAIC)

SAIC, the first regional institution was established in Dhaka in 1988. SAIC serves to network relevant national information centres in Member States with a view to exchanging regionally generated technical information to strengthen agricultural research and development activities. SAIC has brought out several publications which contain information on agricultural institutions in SAARC countries as well as on fisheries, forestry, livestock and crops.

The publications completed by SAIC include: Directory of Agricultural Institutions, Directory of Agricultural Scientists and Technologists and Agricultural Periodicals of the SAARC Countries. It also completed a Bibliography of Women in Agriculture; and a Bibliography of Agro-forestry in the SAARC Region. It maintains databases respectively on Fish Diseases and on Potato Cultivation in the SAARC Region. It also publishes quarterly newsletter highlighting its activities.

During the fifteenth meeting of the Governing Board of SAIC held in Dhaka on 24-26 September 2001, it was recommended that SAIC undertake publication of a

SAARC Journal of Agriculture, a Regional Directory of Plant Genetic Resources, a Handbook on Diseases of Livestock, a Statistical Bulletin of SAARC Agricultural Data and a SAARC Directory of Seed Companies/ Entrepreneurs. The sixteenth meeting of the Board was held in Dhaka on 6-8 October 2002 which while reviewing the completed programmes of 2001 and those planned for 2002, proposed regular and other activities for the year 2003.

SAARC Tuberculosis Centre (STC)

The STC was set up in 1992 in Kathmandu. The main objective of the STC is to work towards the prevention and control of TB in the region by coordinating the efforts of the National TB Programmes of Member States. It serves as a Regional Coordination Centre for National Tuberculosis Control Programmes in the region and functions as a centre for information exchange and related activities by collecting, collating, analysing and disseminating all relevant information regarding the latest developments and findings in the field of tuberculosis in the region and elsewhere. It is also working to establish a networking arrangement among the National Tuberculosis Programmes.

Among its objectives are to initiate, undertake and coordinate research and training in technical, biomedical, operational and other aspects related to tuberculosis control programmes in the region; to ensure adequate supply at low cost of antituberculosis drugs and other related supplies in all the Member States; to monitor incidence, prevalence and emergence of drug resistant strains of tuberculosis in the region; to promote action on issues relating to HIV related tuberculosis in the SAARC region; and to carry out any other functions related to tuberculosis at the directive of the Technical Committee on Social Development.

A project proposal for the enhancement of the STC's capacity to deal with HIV/AIDS related tuberculosis under the SAARC-CIDA Memorandum of Understanding has been prepared and a Regional Strategy on TB and HIV/AIDS Control is being formulated.

The STC has developed a format for collection of information related to tuberculosis and HIV/AIDS from SAARC Member States. The Centre also publishes a newsletter twice a year which includes its activities, special articles and technical information on TB. The STC has been organising seminars, workshops, and training programmes related to TB control. Experts and TB Programme Managers are kept informed about recent developments in the field of TB control in and around the region, including information from WHO. The Centre also organises meetings of National TB Programme Managers of Member States to discuss the problems faced during implementation of programmes. SAARC Documentation Centre (SDC)

The SDC was established in New Delhi in May 1994. The SAARC Documentation System (SDS) comprises the central facility i.e. SDC and its sub-units in Member States which act as the Centre's repositories. In fulfilling the need for ready access to information, the SDC focuses on data in Member States and international databases in the areas of biological, physical, chemical, engineering and life sciences as well as in development matters.

The SDC has undertaken several training courses in the fields of library science and information technology. A twoyear Master Degree Course on "Associateship in

Information Science" has also been included in its regular activities. The SDC is currently engaged in a project on creation of a Database on Training Facilities in the SAARC region. The Eighth Meeting of the Governing Board was held in New Delhi in November 2002.

SAARC Meteorological Research Centre (SMRC) The SMRC was inaugurated on 2 January 1995 in Dhaka. The Centre concentrates primarily on the research aspects of weather forecasting and monitoring. In addition to monitoring weather phenomena, the Centre is also engaged in developing a networking system among Member States.

The Centre's ongoing activities include collating data from national meteorological services and other up-to-date climatological information for the compilation of a Directory of Meteorological Professionals and Technicians in South Asia; bringing out newsletters regarding its programmes; and collating required meteorological data from sources outside the region for its research programmes. The eighth meeting of the Governing Board of SMRC took place in Dhaka in October 2002.

SAARC Human Resources Development Centre (SHRDC)

The SAARC Human Resources Development Centre (SHRDC) has been established in Islamabad with an objective to undertake research, training and dissemination of information on human resources development issues. At its second meeting, the Governing Board finalised the terms of reference, budget/programme of activities, administrative/financial rules and other functional aspects of the Centre. The third meeting, which was held in Islamabad in October

2002, proposed its programme budget along with institutional cost. This meeting also identified for the first time programme activities to be undertaken during the year 2003. These activities include:

— development of a database in the areas of education, health, gender, poverty, children and environment;

— preparation of a directory of HRD institutions in SAARC countries;

— development of a SHRDC website; publication of a SHRDC newsletter; and

— holding of a training programme on poverty alleviation.

Proposed Regional Centres

In addition to the above regional centres already functioning in various fields under the SAARC umbrella, establishment of the following centres is under consideration:

— SAARC Cultural Centre in Kandy (Sri Lanka)

— SAARC Coastal Zone Management Centre (Maldives)

— SAARC Information Centre.

Economic Agenda

The acceleration of economic growth is a Charter objective of SAARC. Cooperation in the core economic areas among SAARC Member Countries was initiated following the Study on Trade, Manufactures and Services (TMS), completed in June 1991. The Study considered economic cooperation among the countries of the SAARC region as an inevitable imperative for promoting all-round development of the region. The Council of Ministers at its Ninth Session in Malé in July 1991 endorsed the Study and established the Committee on Economic Cooperation (CEC) comprising Commerce/ Trade Secretaries of Member States.

Committee on Economic Cooperation (CEC) The CEC is mandated to formulate and oversee implementation of specific measures, policies and programmes to strengthen and enhance intra-regional cooperation in the fields of trade and economic relations. With the creation of the CEC, regional economic cooperation was formally institutionalised as an integral component of the SAARC process.

Over the years, the CEC has emerged as the central group within SAARC addressing economic and trade-related issues. It has provided recommendations and guidance in identifying new areas of cooperation as well as considering reports of specially constituted groups. Its specific functions include analysing inter-regional and global developments which impact on intra-regional cooperation; evolving joint strategies and common approaches at international forums; and recommending policies and measures for promoting intra-regional trade, joint ventures, industrial complementarity and investments. The mandate of the CEC covers areas ranging from quality control, standards and measurements to customs cooperation, harmonisation of documentations and procedures, preferential trading arrangements and rules of origin, and the transition from the SAARC Preferential Trading Arrangement (SAPTA) to the South Asian Free Trade Area (SAFTA). The recommendations of the CEC are submitted through the Standing Committee to higher SAARC bodies, namely the Council of Ministers and the Summit. Eleven Meetings of the CEC have been held so far, the last one being in Kathmandu in October 2002.

Meetings of Commerce Ministers

Recognising the important role economic cooperation plays in South Asia and the need to give policy directives at ministerial level, the first meeting of SAARC Commerce Ministers was held in New Delhi in January 1996. Since then, two more meetings of the Commerce Ministers were held in Islamabad (April 1998) and Dhaka (February 1999). These meetings focused on enlarging the scope and coverage of regional economic cooperation. Meetings of Commerce Ministers were also held to evolve common positions on issues before WTO Ministerial Meetings.

SAARC Preferential Trading Arrangement (SAPTA) The agreement on SAPTA was signed on 11 April 1993. It entered into force on 7 December 1995. So far, four rounds of trade negotiations were concluded under SAPTA covering over 5500 commodities. Each round contributed to an incremental trend in the product coverage and the deepening of tariff concessions over previous rounds. The fourth round of trade negotiations under SAPTA was concluded at the Second Meeting of Inter-Governmental Group on Trade Liberalisation held at the SAARC Secretariat on 30 October – 1 November 2002. The Member States are in the process of completing the necessary procedural formalities to give effect to the concessions they have extended in the Fourth Round. The Meeting recommended that till such time as the South

Asian Free Trade Area (SAFTA) is given effect to, the process of trade negotiations under SAPTA may be continued for further trade liberalisation in the region.

The basic principles underlying SAPTA are:

(a) overall reciprocity and mutuality of advantages so as to benefit equitably all Contracting States, taking into account their respective level of economic and industrial development, the pattern of their external trade, and trade and tariff policies and systems;

(b) negotiation of tariff reform step by step, improved and extended in successive stages through periodic reviews;

(c) recognition of the special needs of the Least Developed Contracting States and agreement on concrete preferential measures in their favour; and

(d) inclusion of all products, manufactures and commodities in their raw, semi-processed and processed forms. South Asian Free Trade Area (SAFTA)

The Tenth SAARC Summit in Colombo decided to set up a Committee of Experts to draft a comprehensive treaty framework for creating a free trade area within the region, taking into consideration the asymmetries in development within the region and bearing in mind the need to fix realistic and achievable targets. Four Meetings of the Committee of Experts have since been held.

The Institute of Policy Studies (IPS) of Sri Lanka was appointed by the Secretary-General as a Consultant to conduct a Study on Implications to the Member States of Progression from SAPTA to SAFTA. The Study has since been completed and is currently being examined by

Member States. The draft of the SAFTA Treaty Framework is expected to be finalized in the next Meeting of the Committee of Experts. The process has benefited from inputs by the South Asian corporate sector as well.

The Eleventh Summit held in Kathmandu in January 2002 provided further impetus to the regional economic cooperation to give effect to the shared aspirations for a more prosperous South Asia. At the same Summit, the Leaders agreed to accelerate cooperation in the core areas of trade, finance and investment to realise the goal of an integrated South Asian economy in a step-by-step manner. They also agreed to the vision of a phased and planned process eventually leading to a South Asian Economic Union.

Trade Facilitation Measures

Action is underway on a series of practical measures aimed at trade facilitation such as a Regional Agreement on the Promotion and Protection of Investments in the SAARC Region, a SAARC Arbitration Council and a Regional Agreement on the Avoidance of Double Taxation. In 1996, a Group on Customs Cooperation was set up and entrusted with a mandate, inter-alia, to harmonise customs rules and regulations; to simplify documentation and procedural requirements; to upgrade infrastructure facilities; and to provide training facilities. A Customs Action Plan has also been drawn up. A Consultant on Customs Matters is to be appointed by the Secretary-General shortly.

A Standing Group on Standards, Quality Control and Measurements was also established by the SAARC

Commerce Ministers in May 1998. The Group held its first meeting in New Delhi in June 1999 to identify how national standards may be harmonised and regional standards agreed upon. The meeting also agreed on key elements of the Regional Action Plan on Standards, Quality Control and Measurements. The Standing Group met for the second time in New Delhi in February 2002 and considered a proposal for collaborative arrangement with the German national metrology institute, Physikalisch-Technische Bundesanstalt (PTB). The text of the Draft between SAARC and PTB is under consideration of Member States.

Collective Positions on Trade Issues at Multilateral Fora

The Tenth Summit reiterated its resolve to promote the articulation of joint positions in multilateral fora. The Summit also took note of emerging issues relating to copyright, patents and marketing franchises, including those on food grains, plants and herbs indigenous to South Asia, which required a collective response to preserve the bio-resources from unregulated commercial exploitation. A series of consultations held prior to the WTO Ministerial Conferences resulted in the enunciation of the common SAARC positions through Joint Statements issued by the SAARC Commerce Ministers.

At the Eleventh Summit, while recognising the important role that trade plays in advancing the overall development of a country, thus contributing to an equitable and sustainable world order, the Leaders called for early realisation of a rule-based and non-discriminatory world trade regime. In this context, they appreciated the positive elements of the Fourth WTO

Ministerial Conference held in Doha and called upon the developed countries to fulfill their commitments to address the particular concerns and needs of the developing and the least-developed countries. The Leaders also instructed the Committee on Economic Cooperation (CEC) to discuss and evaluate decisions of the Doha Conference in order to evolve better coordinated positions among the Member States on all WTO issues. They further stressed the need to intensify coordination among SAARC Member Countries and to prepare for advancing the common interest in the region at the Fifth WTO Conference in Cancún on 10-14 September 2003.

Regular consultations on WTO matters are also conducted among SAARC Permanent Representatives based in Geneva.

Enhancement of Institutional Capacity

The Tenth Summit recognised the need to strengthen individual financial systems of the SAARC countries through enhancement of their institutional capacity and surveillance mechanisms as well as through closer consultations on and coordination of macroeconomic policies where appropriate. In order to enhance SAARC's collective capacity in respect of policy analysis with specific emphasis on international financial, monetary, trade and investment issues, meetings of finance officials of SAARC countries including regular consultations between Governors of Central Banks have been held within the framework of SAARCFINANCE - a grouping of the Central Banks of Member States.

In addition, as mandated by the Tenth Summit, a Network of Researchers on Global Financial and Economic Issues has been set up to identify, analyse and help SAARC face up to global financial and economic developments affecting the region. The Network which brings together the private sector, central banks, planning ministries, research institutes and eminent economists nominated by Governments has been working on an immediate and long-term research agenda to help identify areas of common concern as also new areas of cooperation among Member Countries. The Network brings out the South Asia Economic Journal. It has also compiled a Directory of Research Institutes in South Asia focusing on global financial and economic issues.

The Private Sector

The private sector has played an important role in steering the SAARC economic agenda forward. The SAARC Chamber of Commerce and Industry (SCCI), set up in 1992 as a SAARC-recognized Apex Body, has played a significant role in this regard by bringing together the national chambers of commerce and industry of Member States. Its activities range from promoting trade and interaction of the business community within the SAARC region to providing inputs for SAPTA and SAFTA. The SCCI also organises Economic Cooperation Conferences annually in different Member States to focus on building stronger partnership and collaboration between Governments and Industry. At the Eleventh Summit, the Leaders renewed their commitment to encouraging the participation of the private sector and assured their full support for the latter's socially responsible economic initiatives. They appreciated the efforts of the SCCI to promote regional economic cooperation in the spirit of public and private sector partnership. A declaration on Government-Industry Partnership Affirmation was presented by SCCI to the Council prior to the Eleventh Summit.

Trade Fairs

SAARC Trade Fairs organized by the SAARC Chamber of Commerce and Industry (SCCI) are one of the important vehicles for promoting intra-SAARC trade. The first SAARC Trade Fair was held in New Delhi in 1996, the second in Colombo in 1998, the third in Karachi in 2001 and the fourth in Kathmandu in 2002. The fifth SAARC Trade Fair will be held in Bangladesh in December 2003.

Promotion of Organised Tourism and the SAARC Tourism Council

The Second SAARC Summit in Bangalore in 1986 stressed on the importance of the promotion of tourism in South Asia and in this context, emphasized on the need to promote people-to-people contacts in the region.

Subsequently, the SAARC Scheme of Promotion of Organized Tourism was initiated with the objectives of strengthening people-to-people contacts in the region and promoting cooperation in the holding of training programmes, exchange of information and joint-venture investment among Member Countries. It is envisaged that the Scheme would facilitate exchange of organised group tours between the Member Countries with a provision for concessional air fare and arrangement for limited convertibility of foreign exchange through a travel voucher system thereby providing for a new impetus for the promotion of tourism in the region.

In view of the important role of the private sector in the area of tourism, the tourism related activities undertaken by the erstwhile Technical Committee on Tourism were entrusted to the SCCI Tourism Council - a body under the SAARC Chamber of Commerce and Industry. The SCCI Tourism Council fulfils this role under the guidance of the Committee on Economic Cooperation.

At the Eleventh Summit, the Leaders recognised the immense tourism potentials of South Asia and underlined the need to take measures to promote South Asia as a common tourist destination through joint efforts in areas such as upgrading of infrastructure, simplifying air linkages and harmonising administrative procedures, training and joint marketing.

Senior officials dealing with tourism in Member Countries met in New Delhi on 25-26 February 2003 and recommended a number of measures to promote intra-regional tourism.

Social Agenda

The SAARC Charter envisages the acceleration of social progress through active collaboration and mutual assistance among Member States in the social field. Social issues under the broad heading of Health and Population Activities were one of the original five areas of cooperation decided by Member States. The primary focus of the Technical Committee thus set up in 1984 was on maternal and child health, primary health care, disabled and handicapped persons, and combating major diseases in the region such as malaria, leprosy, tuberculosis, diarrhoea, rabies and AIDS.

In the areas of child development and health, SAARC has been closely cooperating with international agencies such as UNICEF with which it signed an MoU in December 1993. The MoU envisages cooperation in implementing the relevant SAARC decisions relating to children through an annual agenda which includes preparation of joint studies, exchange of documentation and monitoring of implementation.

SAARC recognizes that issues related to gender and empowerment of women need to be addressed to promote social development. In this regard, it has an MoU with the United Nations Development Fund for Women (UNIFEM) signed in December 2001 for cooperation in the promotion of gender issues.

Ministerial Conferences have taken place focussing on the social agenda. These include a Ministerial Conference on Women and Family Health (Kathmandu, 1993) and a Ministerial Meeting on Disabled Persons (Islamabad, 1993).

Women

Thirteen meetings have been held of the Technical Committee on Women in Development since gender issues were included under the IPA in 1986. Activities have included pursuing a Regional Plan of Action for Women; publishing the SAARC Solidarity Journals on specific themes on women; highlighting the plight of the Girl Child in South Asia; and holding gender-related workshops, seminars and training programmes.

Concerned over the trafficking of women and children within and between countries, Member Countries signed a Regional Convention on Combating the Crime of Trafficking in Women and Children for Prostitution on 5 January 2002 during the Eleventh Summit held in Kathmandu. The Convention calls for cooperation amongst Member States to effectively deal with the various aspects of prevention, interdiction and suppression of trafficking in women and children for prostitution and for the repatriation and rehabilitation of victims of trafficking. It also calls for the prevention of use of women and children in international prostitution networks, particularly where the countries of SAARC region are the countries of origin, transit and destination.

The Leaders at their Eleventh Summit expressed their collective resolve to treat the trafficking in women and children for commercial sexual exploitation as a criminal offence of a serious nature. Accordingly, they directed the Council of Ministers to (a) take necessary measures to ensure the enjoyment by women and children of their inherent potential, (b) constitute a Task Force to review the status of implementation of past decisions related to the social sector and suggest guidelines for their effective implementation, and © form an advocacy group of prominent women personalities from Member States to prepare and present a broad spectrum of gender issues.

The Leaders also agreed to mobilise necessary resources and to intensify broad-based action to achieve a set of priority goals in improving the social status of women and children, such as (a) establishing a voluntary fund with the contribution from Member States, individuals and donor countries and agencies for the rehabilitation and reintegration of the victims of trafficking, and (b) pursuing and promoting social development through empowerment of women and achieving their full participation in decision making at all levels.

Ministerial Conferences on Women were held in Shillong (1986), Islamabad (1990), Kathmandu (1993) and Dhaka (1995). The Ministerial Conference in Dhaka adopted a "Dhaka Resolution on Women" which was later presented to the Fourth World Conference on Women (Beijing, 1995).

Children

The development and well-being of children is a principal area of cooperation identified by SAARC from its very inception. The objective of building a region-wide consensus on social action for achieving the rights of the child and the goals set for them within the framework of a survival, development and protection strategy was addressed during the three Ministerial Conferences on Children held in Delhi (1986), Colombo (1992) and Rawalpindi (1996). Since a decision of the Second SAARC Summit (Bangalore, 1986) that the survival, protection and development of children be given the highest priority, annual reviews on the Situation of Children in SAARC countries were initiated in 1993 and the last such review was undertaken in 1998. The Reviews have been an important source of ascertaining the status of the well-being of children and monitoring progress thereon.

The Ninth Summit (Male', 1997) gave further impetus to tackling the important issues relating to women and children. It resolved to implement appropriate policies at the national level to achieve the targets and objectives set out in the Rawalpindi Declaration adopted by the Third Ministerial Conference on Children (August, 1996).

Pursuant to the decision of the Ninth Summit, the SAARC Convention on Regional Arrangements on the Promotion of Child Welfare in South Asia was signed on 5 January 2002 during the Eleventh Summit in Kathmandu. The objectives of the Convention include facilitating the development and protection of full potential of the South Asian child, with the understanding of their rights, duties and responsibilities as well as those of others.

In signing the Convention, the Leaders reaffirmed their conviction that children in South Asia deserve urgent and focused attention to enhance the long term and overall progress of the countries in the region. Accordingly, the Summit directed the Council of Ministers, inter-alia, to (a) take necessary measures to ensure the enjoyment by girl child of her inherent potential; and (b) take concrete steps to give priority to investing in children as an effective means for poverty reduction in the long run.

The Summit also agreed to mobilise necessary resources and to intensify broad-based actions to achieve a set of priority goals in improving the status of children, such as polio eradication by 2005; protection of children from mother-tochild transmission of HIV/AIDS; and quality basic education to children. Moreover, the year 1990 was observed as the SAARC Year of the Girl Child and the decade of 1991-2000 was designated as the SAARC Decade of the Girl Child. The decade from 2001 to 2010 is being observed as the SAARC Decade of the Rights of the Child.

Health

Member States have taken a number of initiatives in the area of health care and disease control. Discussions on health issues have highlighted the need for strengthening efforts to combat problems posed by the resurgence of communicable diseases such as malaria and TB, and waterborne diseases, and the emergence of AIDS as a major health hazard.

Arrangements for training and research activities with regional approaches to combat major diseases in the region have been undertaken. A Directory of training programmes in six priority areas, i.e. malaria, tuberculosis, leprosy, diarrhoeal diseases, human rabies, and maternal and child health has been prepared. Member States have also identified Centres to act as focal points on selected diseases.

The SAARC Tuberculosis Centre (STC), established in Kathmandu in 1992 plays an important role in the prevention and control of tuberculosis in the SAARC region by coordinating the efforts of the National TB Control Programmes of the Member Countries. A SAARC project with the Canadian International Development Agency (CIDA) aims to enhance the capacity of the STC to coordinate the joint efforts of the SAARC Countries in meeting a major concern of the region – the combined toll of TB and AIDS.

SAARC has signed an MoU with WHO in August 2000 for mutual cooperation in agreed areas to help Member Countries strive towards the goal of Health for All. Under the MoU, collaboration with the SAARC Tuberculosis Centre and other institutions in South Asia, particularly those active in the control of malaria, tuberculosis and HIV/AIDS is being facilitated. WHO has declared the STC as a WHO Collaborating Centre.

Protection of Environment

The subject of environment has received special attention from the very inception of the Association. Several initiatives have been taken to strengthen cooperation among Member Countries in the protection of environment.

Regional Study on Environment

The Leaders during the Third SAARC Summit (Kathmandu, 1987), deeply concerned over the fast and continuing degradation of the environment including extensive destruction of forests resulting in natural disasters, commissioned the study on the causes and consequences of natural disasters and the protection and preservation of the environment. Accordingly, a Group of Experts with participation from all the SAARC Countries was constituted to prepare the Study. The Group finalized the format of the Study which was completed in 1991. Its main recommendations were endorsed by the Heads of State or Government at their Sixth Summit (Colombo, 1991). The Study contains measures to protect and manage the environment; to strengthen disaster management capabilities; and to evolve implementation mechanisms as outlined in the Study.

Regional Study on the Greenhouse Effect and its Impact on the Region The Fourth SAARC Summit (Islamabad, 1988) while noting with serious concern the extensive damage caused in many SAARC Countries due to unprecedented floods, cyclones and earthquakes, recalled their earlier decision to enhance regional cooperation with a view to strengthening the region's disaster management capabilities. In this context, they urged that a study on the greenhouse effect and its impact on the region be completed to provide a basis for a regional action plan for meaningful cooperation among Member States.

The Fifth SAARC Summit (Male', 1990) noted with satisfaction the methodology recommended for the Study on the Greenhouse Effect and its Impact on the Region. Following meetings of a Group of Experts and a Group of Coordinators, the Study was finalized in 1992. During the Seventh SAARC Summit in Dhaka in 1993, the Leaders recognized that the completion of the Study was a significant step forward in promoting regional cooperation in this vital area. The Study suggested measures in sharing experiences, scientific capabilities and information on climate change, and forging global collaboration in monitoring climatology, sea level rise, natural disaster, technology transfer and finance.

Ministerial Meetings

In pursuance of the decision of the Heads of State/ Government during the Sixth SAARC Summit in December 1991, the First SAARC Environment Ministers' Conference was held in New Delhi (8-9 April 1992) which deliberated upon the issues related to the United Nations Conference on Environment and Development (UNCED). Since then, five Ministerial Conferences on Environment have taken place.

The New Delhi meeting (April 2-3, 1997) of the SAARC Environment Ministers culminated in the adoption of 'The 1997 New Delhi Declaration' of Environment Ministers on a common SAARC position before the UNGA Special Session on the implementation of Agenda 21.

The Environment Ministers' Conference (Male', October 15-16, 1997) reviewed the recommendations of the SAARC Study on the Greenhouse Effect and its Impact on the Region, and decided to identify some priority areas for immediate action for enhanced partnership and cooperation. The Ministers while reviewing the recommendations of the SAARC Study on the Causes and Consequences of the Natural Disasters and the Protection and Preservation of the Environment viewed that their follow-up had been very slow inspite of some efforts to implement them at the national level. They, therefore, decided to identify some priority areas for immediate action in order to provide the framework for enhanced partnership and cooperation in them. The measures adopted for the implementation of the recommendations of the Study are reflected in the Male' Declaration of SAARC Environment Ministers.

During the same meeting, the Ministers formulated a common SAARC position on Climate Change for presentation at the third meeting of the Conference of the Parties to the UN Framework Convention on Climate Change held in Kyoto, Japan during December 1997. Recognising the need for sound environmental protection regime in the region, it was agreed to conduct a feasibility study on a Regional Treaty on Environment in the context of existing international conventions.

The Fourth SAARC Environment Ministers' Conference (Colombo, 30 October – 01 November 1998) adopted the Colombo Declaration on Environment for a Common Environment Programme. They also formulated a common position on Climate Change for presentation at the Buenos Aires Meeting.

The Ministers at their Fifth Meeting (Thimphu, 10-11 August 2002) noted that the proposal on the establishment of a Coastal Zone Management Centre would be considered at the Expert Group Meeting to be hosted by Maldives. The Ministers also formulated a common SAARC position for presentation at the World Summit for Sustainable Development (Johannesburg, 27 August – 4 September 2002). Pursuant to the former decision, the Expert Group Meeting to Consider the Feasibility on Setting Up a SAARC Coastal Zone Management Centre was held in Male' on 16-17 December 2002.

Plan of Action on Environment

The Third Meeting of Environment Ministers (Male', 1997) adopted the SAARC Plan of Action on Environment. The Action Plan is based on the recommendations of the two Studies outlined above. The Plan evaluates the status of SAARC cooperation in the field of environment, identifies the concerns of Member States at regional and global levels and sets out parameters and modalities for enhanced cooperation. Member States are called upon to mobilize financial resources from regional and international organizations.

The main responsibility for the implementation of the Action Plan rests with Member States. Each Member

State is called upon to prepare a National Action Plan on Environment. In order to facilitate the implementation of SAARC Plan of Action on Environment, Member States are required to submit to the Secretariat National State of the Environment Reports. A SAARC State of the Environment Reports will then be prepared based on these reports. The SAARC Plan of Action also highlights the need of a Regional Treaty on Environment, which will ensure a sound environment protection regime for the region. The year 1992 was observed as the 'SAARC Year of the Environment.'

The Colombo Declaration for a Common Environment Programme The Fourth Environment Ministers' Meeting adopted the Common Environment Programme (Colombo, 1998). The Programme took into account various major international instruments and declarations on environment and stressed on the importance of enhanced cooperation in sharing information in the region to promote effective management of the environment.

The programme provides for compilation of a regional directory of scientific and technological institutions in the field of environment and state-of-the-art report on eco-friendly technologies; promotion of coastal zone management; promotion of disaster management and disaster prevention; adoption of a regional framework for protecting all genetic resources and for the exchange of information on enabling legal measures; and focusing on a single theme in each of the future meetings of the Ministers to highlight specific environmental projects within the region. The theme for the year 2002/2003 is "Contribution of Youth to Environment."

The Fourth Environment Ministers' Meeting (Colombo, 1998) also considered the feasibility of establishing a SAARC Forestry Centre. The Meeting decided that Member States furnish a list of national forestry institutions. The Secretariat, after receiving the lists from Member Countries will consult them on the modalities of operation of such a regional centre.

Agreements, Conventions and Legal Issues

Agreement on Establishing the SAARC Food Security Reserve

During the Third SAARC Summit (Kathmandu, 1987), an Agreement on Establishing the SAARC Food Security Reserve was signed. The Agreement, which came into force on 12 August 1988, provides for a reserve of food grains to meet emergencies in Member Countries. The Reserve stood at 241,580 tonnes as of January 2002.

The SAARC Food Security Reserve Board (SFSRB) comprising representatives from Member Countries meets once a year. The Board normally meets at the same place and time as the Standing Committee, preceding the annual Summit. The Board reports to the Council of Ministers.

The main function of the Board is to undertake a periodic review and assessment of the food situation and prospects in the region taking into account factors like production, consumption, trade, prices, quality and stocks of food grains. A special meeting of the Board held in Kathmandu in April 2001 dwelt upon the possibility of instituting more practical measures for facilitating the use of the Reserve during emergencies.

The Ninth Meeting of the Board held in Islamabad in December 2002 reviewed, amongst others, the implementation of recommendations of the Eighth Meeting of the Board and identified institutions/ organizations in Member States to be contacted in case of emergency requirements for withdrawal from the Reserve.

Regional Convention on Suppression of Terrorism The SAARC Regional Convention on Suppression of Terrorism signed during the Third SAARC Summit in Kathmandu in November 1987 came into force on 22 August 1988 following its ratification by all Member States. The Convention provides for a regional approach to wellestablished principles of international law in respect of terrorist offences. Under its provisions, Member States are committed to extradite or prosecute alleged terrorists. Regional cooperation is also envisaged in preventive action to combat terrorism through exchange of information, intelligence and expertise.

As a follow up to the Convention, the SAARC Terrorist Offences Monitoring Desk (STOMD) has been established in Colombo to collate, analyze and disseminate information about the terrorist incidences, tactics, strategies and methods.

The SAARC Legal Experts, who met in Kandy, Sri Lanka in June 1999, while reviewing the progress in the implementation of the regional Convention considered the issue of updating it in the light of developments in the international legal field. They viewed that the Convention provided for an interim regime to cope with international developments in the field.

At the Eleventh SAARC Summit in Kathmandu in January 2002, the Heads of State or Government reiterated their determination to prevent and suppress terrorism in all its forms and manifestations and reaffirmed their commitment to the Convention on Suppression of Terrorism.

Pursuant to the decision of the Twenty-second Session of the Council of Ministers held in Kathmandu in January 2002, a meeting of Legal Advisors of SAARC Member States in May 2002 in Sri Lanka addressed legal issues of interest to the region in the light of recent developments in the field of suppression of terrorism. The meeting, inter-alia,recognized the importance of enacting enabling legislation in Member States as required by the Convention. Taking into account the SAARC Convention on Terrorism and the qualitative change in the international legal regime following the events of 11 September 2001, the Meeting deliberated on the question of a possible review of the Convention in order to incorporate the recent developments in the international regime to combat terrorism. It was agreed that the objective of such a review would not be to reopen the Convention, but to determine whether any additional instrument, for instance by way of a protocol, was required to supplement the Convention. A meeting of senior officials from Member States assisted by legal experts is to be held in Colombo shortly for this purpose.

Regional Convention on Narcotic Drugs and Psychotropic Substances The Convention was signed in Male' during the Fifth SAARC Summit in November 1990. The Convention came into force on 15 September 1993.

The Convention calls for the promotion of regional cooperation among Member States in both law enforcement and demand reduction. It also provides for measures for mutual legal assistance among Member States in investigation, prosecution and judicial proceedings in respect of drug offences.

The SAARC Drug Offences Monitoring Desk (SDOMD) has been established in Colombo to collate, analyze and disseminate information on drug related offences in Member Countries. Cooperation among Drug Law Enforcement Agencies and Officers is being facilitated through short-term activities such as seminars, training courses etc. Since the establishment of the SDOMD, information on drug offences received from Liaison Officers of Member States is being exchanged, collated and analyzed at the Desk. A Joint Meeting of the SAARC Drug Offences Monitoring Desk (SDOMD) and Drug Liaison Officers of SAARC countries held in Colombo in October 2002 reviewed the existing procedures and constraints, and suggested practical measures for enhancing information coverage. Recommendations were also made to work out joint programmes with UNDP, Colombo Plan, JICA and JICWEC to train operational level officials in identifying chemicals including precursors and strengthening SAARC drug control measures.

A Workshop on policy formulation in the field of Precursor Control in the SAARC region was held at the Secretariat in August 2001 in collaboration with the United Nations Drug Control Programme (UNDCP). The workshop, among others, urged SAARC Member States to enact exclusive legislation for the regulation and control of precursor chemicals. It called on UNDCP to assist the Governments concerned in drawing up the necessary legislation on request.

The Meeting of Legal Advisers of Member States in Colombo in May 2002 recognized the need for harmonization of domestic legislations in respect of the Convention. During the Meeting, attention was paid to the aspect of harmonizing the sanction regime.

SAARC Convention on Preventing and Combating Trafficking in Women and Children for Prostitution

At the Ninth SAARC Summit in May 1997, the Heads of State or Government expressed grave concern over the trafficking of women and children within and between countries. They pledged to coordinate their efforts and to take effective measures to address this problem. They decided that existing legislation in Member States should be strengthened and strictly enforced to simplify repatriation procedures for victims of trafficking. They also decided that the feasibility of a Regional Convention in combating the crime of trafficking in women and children for prostitution be examined by the relevant Technical Committee.

The SAARC Convention on Preventing and Combating Trafficking in Women and Children for Prostitution was signed on 5 January 2002 at the Eleventh SAARC Summit in Kathmandu. The Heads of State or Government while welcoming the signing of the Convention expressed their collective resolve to treat the trafficking in women and children for commercial sexual exploitation as a criminal offence of a serious nature. They also recommended that the feasibility of establishing a Regional Fund for Rehabilitation of Victims of Trafficking in Women and Children for Prostitution on a voluntary basis might be explored. The Convention will enter into force upon ratification by all Member States.

SAARC Convention on Regional Arrangements for the Promotion of Child Welfare in South Asia The Convention was signed on 5 January 2002 during the Eleventh Summit in Kathmandu. The objective of the Convention is to facilitate the development and protection of full potential of the South Asian child, with the understanding of their rights, duties and responsibilities. The Convention will enter into force upon ratification by all Member States.

Coordination of Positions on Multilateral Legal Issues The subject of Intellectual Property (IP) received a collective South Asian policy focus for the first time during the Tenth SAARC Summit in Colombo. This was in the context of the Summit addressing the need to evolve collective responses to global economic and financial challenges in general. It was agreed that the Intellectual Property issues needed to be addressed through regional cooperation.

WIPO in cooperation with SAARC countries has held four sub-regional forums for Intellectual Property cooperation in Colombo (1998), Kathmandu (1999), Dhaka (2001) and Thimpu (2002). The objectives of these forums were to highlight the importance of Intellectual Property to SAARC countries and its ever-increasing impact on technological, cultural, social and economic progress in the region, to promote and foster closer cooperation and understanding in the field of IP; and to provide an opportunity for consideration of IP issues in the region.

The Forums underlined the importance of the continued involvement of SAARC in the field of protection of traditional knowledge, genetic resources and folklore. Intellectual property issues have emerged in a wide range of policy areas, including food and agriculture, biological diversity, protection of environment, cultural policy, and trade and economic development.

The SAARC-WIPO Forums have identified the need to harmonize existing national principles and rules within South Asia relating to Intellectual Property protection; to develop common positions and approaches in international forums including WTO; to strengthen decision making, working methods and procedures within the region in the field; and to evolve and harmonize international norms of protection in areas of interest to the region, particularly traditional intellectual treasures.

Another important area of focus of the Forums was small and medium-sized enterprises (SMEs). It was recognized that SMEs play a vital role in employment creation, investment and trade, and are a major source of innovation and technological development contributing to the economic growth of countries in the region. The Forums underscored that a strong and effective Intellectual Property rights protection regime, characterized by efficient enforcement, would provide a big boost to creativity and innovation. These also appreciated the value of public-private sector cooperation in ensuring enforcement of Intellectual Property rights through an effective inter-agency coordination and multi-disciplinary approach.

Protection of SAARC Logo and Nomenclature

Pursuant to the decision of the Third Special Session of the Standing Committee held in Colombo in August

2001, the Secretariat has registered its logo and nomenclature with WIPO under the International Convention on the Protection of Industrial Property (Paris Convention) in order to prevent the use of SAARC logo and nomenclature by unauthorized persons, groups and commercial entities. Member States are committed to taking action to prevent the unauthorized use of the logo and the nomenclature of SAARC and the violation of copyrights of its publications.

SAARC Funds

The South Asian Development Fund (SADF)

The idea of establishing a South Asian Development Fund (SADF) was mooted at the Sixth SAARC Summit in Colombo in December 1991 to mobilise the global surpluses for development of South Asia.

The basic objective of SADF was to provide finances for industrial development, poverty alleviation, protection of environment, balance of payments support, and promotion of economic projects in the region. SADF was established in 1996 with the merger of the two erstwhile Funds: the SAARC Fund for Regional Projects (SFRP) and the SAARC Regional Fund (SRF).

SADF has three Windows for :

(i) identification and development of projects;

(ii) institutional and human resources development projects; and

(iii) social and infrastructural development projects.

SADF has provided funding support (under Window-I) for feasibility studies in respect of 16 approved projects of which 12 have already been completed.

The Governing Board at its sixth meeting in Male' submitted proposals for creation of a substantially larger core capital base for consideration of Member States. Its current core capital base stands at US $ 5.8 million. Pursuant to a decision of the Eleventh Summit to make SADF operational for poverty alleviation by utilising the existing funds, the Secretary-General has come up with a few priority regional poverty alleviation project ideas, which were placed before the seventh Governing Board Meeting of SADF held in Kathmandu in September 2002.

The SAARC-Japan Special Fund

The SAARC-Japan Special Fund was established pursuant to a Memorandum of Understanding signed in Kathmandu on 27 September 1993 between SAARC and the Government of Japan.

The Fund, established with contributions of the Government of Japan, consists of two components. Component-I is to be used to finance selected programmes/activities identified and managed by SAARC. Component-II is for the programmes/activities administered by the Government of Japan.

A large number of seminars, workshops and training programmes have been held so far with resources from the SAARC-Japan Special Fund covering a variety of subjects relating to agriculture and rural development, health, telecommunications, science and technology, education, social and economic issues and the role of media.

Promotion of Human Resources Development

Meetings on Cultural Affairs

The Tenth Summit recognised the profound cultural continuum of South Asia as a historical basis for sustaining harmonious relations among the peoples of the region and welcomed the offer of Sri Lanka to host a meeting Ministers of Cultural Affairs with the objective, inter-alia, establishing a South Asian Cultural Centre to promote the distinctive arts of the region. A preparatory meeting of the Secretaries of Cultural Affairs was held in Colombo November 2001, which recommended practical measures, among others, for protection, conservation and maintenance of cultural and pilgrimage sites; development of archaeology and museology; encouragement of contemporary arts and culture; engaging the corporate sector and non-state organisations in cultural activities; and developing cooperative links with UN and other regional institutions. The Meeting the Cultural Affairs Ministers was held in Colombo on 5-February 2003.

Film and Cultural Festivals

Sri Lanka hosted the first ever SAARC Film Festival September 1999. On that occasion, three seminars were also held on different aspects of the South Asian cinema including on film as cultural expression, film marketing and distribution, and the future of the film industry. In order to strengthen cultural ties among Member States, the Technical Committee on Human Resources Development (Colombo, November 2002) recommended the holding of the second SAARC Cultural Festival in Bangladesh in 2003.

SAARC Consortium of Open and Distance Learning (SACODiL)

In accordance with the decision of the Tenth Summit, the Vice Chancellors of Open Universities met in Colombo in January 1999 and made recommendations for the establishment of SACODiL to strengthen cooperation in the joint development of educational programmes, credit transfers, and promotion of equal opportunities and access to knowledge. The proposal was endorsed by the Twenty-sixth Session of the Standing Committee (Nuwara Eliya, March 1999). The Council of Ministers at its Twenty-second Session approved the convening of the second meeting of the Vice Chancellors of Open Universities/Heads of Distance Learning Institutions of SAARC Member States to review the proposal for the establishment of SACODiL in the light of certain observations made by the Standing Committee while endorsing the proposal.

The meeting of Vice Chancellors of Open

Universities/Heads of National Distance Learning Institutions held in New Delhi on 2-3 December 2002 decided to operate SACODiL through a rotational Secretariat till arrangements were made to establish a permanent Secretariat. The rotational Secretariat will act as a central point for correspondence, maintaining SACODiL records, monitoring the progress of assignments, convening meetings, taking follow-up action and any other functions conferred upon it by the Board of Governors.

The meeting decided to establish the Board of Governors of SACODiL comprising the Vice Chancellors of National Open Universities or Heads of major open and distance learning institutions or educational bodies. The first meeting of the Governing Board of SACODiL is expected to be held in Bangladesh in 2003.

SAARC Chairs, Fellowships and Scholarships Scheme

The SAARC Chairs, Fellowships and Scholarships Scheme was instituted in 1987 with the aim of providing increased cross-fertilisation of ideas through greater interaction among students, scholars and academics in the SAARC countries. The Standing Committee at its Twenty-seventh Session while recognising the importance of the Scheme for Member States decided to hold a workshop in Nepal to recommend means of more effective implementation of the Scheme. Pursuant to the above decision, the second meeting of the Technical Committee on Human Resources Development (Colombo, November 2002) considered the recommendations on operational modalities of the SAARC Chairs, Fellowships and Scholarships Scheme as proposed by the Workshop held in Kathmandu on 22-23 October 2002. The revised Scheme would become operational once it is approved by the Standing Committee.

SAARC Youth Awards Scheme (SYAS)

The SAARC Youth Awards Scheme was established in 1996. The aim of the Scheme is to provide recognition to outstanding young talents and to encourage the overall development of youth in the region. An award is given to a young person who has excelled in a particular field of activity. The first and second SAARC Youth Awards were presented in 1997 and 1998 for "Outstanding Social Service in Community Welfare" and "New Inventions and Discoveries" respectively. The third Award presented in 2001 was for "Creative Photography: South Asian Diversity." The fourth Award for the year 2002 on the theme "Outstanding contribution to protect the Environment" will be presented at the Twenty-fourth Session of the Council of Ministers to be held in Pakistan.

The SAARC Youth Award consists of a cash prize of US$ 1500, a gold medal and a citation.

SAARC Meteorological Awards

A recommendation for instituting an Annual Regional Award for Young Scientists was made by the Working Group on Meteorology at its second meeting in New Delhi as early as December 1982. The Award includes a citation, a bronze medal and an amount equivalent to US$ 500. Up to now, 14 Young Scientists have received the Award. SAARC also instituted a separate Award for Senior Scientists in 1997. The purpose of these awards is to encourage excellence in research analysis and outstanding publications in the meteorological field.

SAARC Award

Recently it has been decided to institute a SAARC Award. The Award shall carry a sum of US$ 8000 together with a medal and a letter of citation. The Award will be conferred on individuals and organizations for the most outstanding work within the region in the fields of peace, development, poverty alleviation and regional cooperation. The operational modalities and other details of the Award are being worked out.

Communications, Information and Media

Communications Ministers' Conferences

During the Ninth SAARC Summit (Malé, May 1997), the Heads of State or Government noted that inadequate communications facilities amongst the Member States were a major hindrance to closer economic cooperation. They stressed on the importance of developing infrastructure and adequate communications networks among Member Countries to reinforce the process of economic cooperation. In this context, they highlighted the need for the simplification of complex documentation procedures and transactional software to facilitate economic interaction across the region.

Pursuant to the above decision, the First SAARC Communications Ministers' Conference was held in Colombo in May 1998. It adopted a Plan of Action on Telecommunications to give impetus to the telecommunications sector in the region. The Plan of Action, inter-alia, calls for reduction of telecom tariffs within the SAARC region to the lowest extent feasible; establishment of special rates for transiting regional traffic; promotion of country direct services, calling cards, cellular roaming and liberalised leased lines; cooperation among regulatory authorities; exchange of information on telecommunications standards; and development of human resources in the telecom sector.

The Plan of Action also calls for evolving a common position on issues of regional concern on telecommunications at international fora. The Tenth SAARC Summit welcoming the results of the first conference noted that technological advances were making telecommunications an important medium for socioeconomic development by developing commercial and business relations as well as promoting people-to-people contacts. The Summit directed speedy implementation of the Plan of Action.

The Second Communications Ministers' Conference to be held in Pakistan in 2003 is expected to review the status of implementation of the Plan of Action.

Meetings of Information Ministers

Recognising the importance of exchange of information and its dissemination amongst Member Countries, the Council of Ministers at its Seventeenth Session (New Delhi, December 1996) called for the convening of a Meeting of SAARC Information Ministers. The first meeting of the SAARC Information Ministers was held in Dhaka in 1998, which adopted the Plan of Action on Information and Media.

The Plan of Action identified a number of activities to be undertaken by Member States, inter-alia, to ensure a free flow of information, newspapers, periodicals, books and other publications; to increase cooperation amongst news agencies of SAARC countries; to facilitate easier travel for media persons within the region; to set up a SAARC recognised Regional Media Forum; to hold annual conferences of editors and journalists; to promote regular exchanges of TV/Radio programmes; to train media persons; to evolve guidelines on transnational satellites; to establish a SAARC satellite; and to consider setting up a SAARC Information Centre as well as a SAARC Media Development Fund.

The Tenth SAARC Summit approved the Plan of Action on Media and Information and called for concerted endeavours for the promotion of practical programmes among South Asian countries in the field of information and media.

The Second Meeting of the SAARC Information Ministers (Islamabad, March 2002) while reviewing the status of implementation of the Dhaka Plan of Action, proposed to set up a SAARC Media Development Fund to promote media linkage within the region to: evolve a SAARC recognized Regional Media Forum; develop model guidelines on transnational satellite broadcasting in the region; establish a SAARC Information Centre; and project and strengthen the South Asian identity beyond the region. The Ministers agreed to convene annual Conferences of Editors and Working Journalists as well as to offer training opportunities for journalists in Member Countries. The Ministers also reviewed the functioning of the SAVE Committee. The proposal of Pakistan to institute a SAARC Award on Folk Music was welcomed by the Ministers.

SAARC Audio-Visual Exchange (SAVE) Programme The SAARC Audio Visual Exchange (SAVE) Committee aimed at increasing the awareness of each other among the peoples of the region and disseminating information about Member Countries was established by the Council of Ministers at its Third Session (New Delhi, June 1987). The Committee has been entrusted with the task of producing and implementing the SAVE Programmes.

The twenty-first meeting of the SAVE Committee (Thimphu, January 2003) finalized radio and TV programmes on various themes for broadcast and telecast on national channels of Radio and TV. The Committee recognized the usefulness of SAARC Radio Music Festival that was held in November 2002 to promote regional culture. It decided to air Radio and TV Music Festivals during the first week and last week of November 2003 respectively.

The SAVE programmes include joint productions on thematic issues such as the Environment, Disabled Persons, Youth, Literacy, Participatory Governance, Safe and Clean Water, and Mountains and Hills. For 2003, the Committee decided to hold Sixth and Seventh SAARC TV Quizzes in Nepal (25 March) and Pakistan (October) respectively.

Similarly, the Fifth SAARC Radio Quiz would take place in New Delhi by end of July. The participation for both the Radio and TV quizzes for 2003 will be at the level of students pursuing bachelors degree studies. While deliberating on the Quiz programmes, it also felt the need to consider new formats such as debates, elocution, youth shows, dramas etc.

Meetings of Heads of National TV and Radio Organisations The Plan of Action on Media and Information called for annual meetings of the Heads of TV/Radio Organisations of Member Countries. Accordingly, the first meeting took place in New Delhi in November 1999, which reviewed the activities of the SAVE Committee and made recommendations to improve the quality of SAVE programmes. Similarly, the second meeting in Islamabad in January 2003 decided that a weekly Radio news entitled "SAARC News" of 5-10 minutes duration as well as a monthly programme of 15 minutes entitled "SAARC Roundup" for TV would go on air from February. This was decided as per the directives of the SAARC Information Ministers, who emphasised on daily exchange of TV and Radio news among Member Countries.

The second meeting also reviewed the progress in the implementation of the Plan of Action on Media and Information which was adopted by Information Ministers with the objective to encourage free flow of information and to strengthen cooperation in the field of media. Among new projects, the meeting decided to organize a Children's Video Film Festival in May 2003. Apart from the above, the meeting discussed a paper by India on developing music archives of SAARC region. The meeting also decided that SAVE Committee produce a video documentary entitled "SAARC in New Millennium."

SAARC Information Centre

The SAARC Plan of Action on Media and Information adopted by the Information Ministers at their first meeting in Dhaka in 1998 calls for the establishment of a SAARC Information Centre. This was approved by the Tenth Summit. The successive meetings of various SAARC bodies have given due emphasis on the subject. In this context, while appreciating the SAARC Secretariat's efforts for dissemination of information on SAARC and taking note of the existing mechanisms for publicity and projection of SAARC activities within and outside the region, the SAARC Information Ministers at their second meeting urged the establishment of a SAARC Information Center with a view to reaching to a wider audience in an effective manner.

Pursuant to the above directives, the Second Meeting of the Heads of TV and Radio Organisations decided to hold an Expert Group Meeting in Pakistan in mid-2003 to work out the technical details of the proposed Centre. The Expert Group Report will be

considered by the third meeting of the SAARC Information Ministers to be held in New Delhi.

SAARC Publications

The SAARC Secretariat has issued a series of cost-free and priced publications to serve a growing demand for information on SAARC activities. The Secretariat also issues a newsletter entitled "SAARC NEWS" which reports on a regular basis on activities of the Association and measures of regional cooperation in South Asia. The list of SAARC publications is included at the end of this publication.

SAARC Website

Recognizing the importance of dissemination of information by improved means of communications technologies, the SAARC Secretariat has expanded its website through a user-friendly surfing touch. The website contains general information on SAARC and Member Countries as well as on the publications of the SAARC Secretariat. The website also includes Press Releases of the Secretariat, key statements made at the SAARC events and news about the activities of the Association.

Library

The Secretariat maintains a Library within its premises in Kathmandu with a fairly wide collection of books on Member Countries as well as on regional cooperation. The Library is open to the general public during working hours of the Secretariat.

Promotion of People-to-people Linkages

SAARC Leaders have attached high priority to the promotion of people-to-people contacts in the region to strengthen mutual understanding and goodwill among the peoples of South Asia. While SAARC is an inter-governmental Association, successive Summits have emphasised on the importance of promoting people-to-people contacts at all levels outside the State sector. In order to give effect to this concept, a number of initiatives have been taken under the aegis of SAARC.

SAARC Visa Exemption Scheme

In order to facilitate closer and more frequent interaction and cooperation among the peoples of the region, the SAARC Visa Exemption Scheme initiated in 1988 became operational on 1 March 1992.

Under the Scheme, visa requirements are waived for specified categories of persons to travel within the SAARC region. The Scheme was expanded in 1999 following consideration of the recommendations of an Expert Group. At present, categories eligible for visa-free travel under the Scheme include Supreme Court Judges, Members of National Parliaments, Government Ministers, other high level officials of Governments, officials of the SAARC Secretariat and its affiliated bodies, and leading businessmen in the region.

The Association of SAARC Speakers and Parliamentarians The Association of SAARC Speakers and Parliamentarians was formally launched in 1992 in Kathmandu. The Heads of State or Government at their Seventh SAARC Summit (Dhaka, April 1993) welcomed the initiative of the Speakers of Parliaments of SAARC countries in forming the Association.

The Association has met in New Delhi (July 1995), Islamabad (October 1997) and Dhaka (March 1999). This Association enjoys a distinct status within SAARC given the standing of its members as heads of legislative assemblies of SAARC Countries. It was granted recognition directly by the Heads of State or Government.

Recognition of Professional Bodies

SAARC has emphasised the need for enriching and supplementing inter-governmental regional efforts through the encouragement of interaction across the region among professional bodies, the private corporate sector, civil society groups and creative artists to promote socio-economic and cultural development in South Asia.

To further facilitate and acknowledge their work, SAARC has granted formal recognition to these bodies under two categories: SAARC Regional Apex Bodies and SAARC Recognised Bodies.

SAARC Regional Apex Bodies

The following enjoy the status of SAARC Regional Apex Bodies:

SAARC Chamber of Commerce and Industry (SCCI)

The SAARC Chamber of Commerce and Industry (SCCI) was granted the status of a SAARC Regional Apex Body in December 1992. The SCCI brings together the national chambers of commerce and industry of the seven SAARC countries. The SCCI has a permanent Secretariat in Islamabad, Pakistan.

The President of the SCCI is elected for a two-year term in rotation among Member States. SCCI plays a significant role in promoting economic and trade cooperation in the region. It has been active in the promotion of interaction among business communities of the SAARC region.

It organises SAARC Economic Cooperation Conferences on a regular basis. So far, it has held six such Conferences: New Delhi (November 1996), Islamabad (March 1998), Dhaka (February 1999), Malé (January 2000), Kathmandu (February 2001) and Kolkata (March 2003). SCCI has also been organising SAARC Trade Fairs in Member Countries. Accordingly, Trade Fairs have been held in New Delhi (1996), Colombo (1998), Karachi (2001) and Kathmandu (2002). The fifth such fair is to be held in Bangladesh (2003).

SAARCLAW

SAARCLAW consists of members of the legal profession in the SAARC countries. Established in 1991, it was accorded recognition as a SAARC Regional Apex Body in July 1994. Among its objectives are to bring together the legal communities of the region for closer cooperation and to develop law as a source and catalyst of social change for development.

SAARCLAW has so far held nine conferences, the latest in Jaipur, India in September 2002, which coincided with the sixth SAARC Chief Justices' Conference. Leaders of Bar Councils of SAARC Countries also met concurrently. The decisions taken by SAARCLAW relate to the formulation of a draft Regional Convention on Human Rights and the establishment of a SAARC Institute of Legal Sciences.

The central theme of the SAARCLAW Conference was "Law As An Instrument Of Social And Economic Change." A SAARCLAW Seminar on "Money Laundering and Debt Recovery" was held in the Maldives on 1 June 2002. The Executive Council of SAARCLAW on 31 May 2002 approved in principle a proposal to establish a college affiliated with the West Bengal National University of Juridical Sciences (WBNUJS) to offer courses to meet contemporary needs of the legal community. It will focus on areas such as WTO, Intellectual Property, International Arbitration, International Trade, Cyber law, Environmental law, Antitrust laws, Consumer Protection etc.

SAARCLAW also brings out a newsletter and text books on legal issues.

South Asian Federation of Accountants (SAFA) SAFA was established in 1984 with the objective of developing "a coordinated accountancy profession in the region." It was granted recognition as a SAARC Recognised Body in May 1997. It was later elevated to the status of a SAARC Apex Body in January 2002.

Its membership is open to accountancy bodies in South Asia. At present, the Institutes of Chartered Accountants and/or the Institutes of Cost and Management Accountants in Bangladesh, India, Pakistan, Nepal and Sri Lanka are the members of SAFA.

The Fiftieth Assembly of SAFA is scheduled to be held in Colombo in July 2003. Its Secretariat is located in India.

SAARC Recognised Bodies

The following enjoy the status of SAARC Recognised Bodies:

South Asian Association for Regional Cooperation of Architects (SAARCH)

SAARCH was founded in 1991 in Colombo with the objective of assisting the development of national architectural bodies within the South Asian region and providing opportunities for conferences of architects to discuss professional matters. It was accorded SAARC recognition in May 1997. It holds conferences in the region and also publishes a newsletter entitled "SAARCH." The Seventh SAARCH Conference was held in Kathmandu in October 2002. The theme of the Conference was "Heritage Conservation and Architecture of Tourism in the SAARC countries."The SAARCH Secretariat is located in Sri Lanka.

Association of Management Development Institutions (AMDISA)

AMDISA was established in June 1988 for promoting management education and training, and fostering management development activities in the South Asian region. It has brought under its umbrella the leading institutions, both public and private, involved in teaching, training and research in management and development oriented fields. It seeks to combine the best elements of public and private sector management norms and techniques. It was accorded SAARC recognition in May 1997. AMDISA has organized several meetings/ conferences on management development related topics.

AMDISA held its Seventh Forum in the Maldives in April 2002. An AMDISA accreditation workshop was organised in June 2002, which was attended by senior faculty members of business schools in South Asia.

AMDISA has also been actively involved in organising the Global Management Forum 2002 in Bangkok. A Regional Doctoral Fellowship Facilitating Programme is being proposed by AMDISA. Its general office is located in India.

SAARC Federation of University Women (SAARCFUW)

SAARCFUW was established in July 1995 in Colombo with the objectives of, inter-alia, bringing together the university women of the region to promote understanding and cooperation and to contribute to the social upliftment in the region. It was accorded SAARC recognition in May 1997. At present, it has national Chapters in Bangladesh, India, Nepal, Pakistan and Sri Lanka. It publishes a newsletter called SAARCFUW.

The Secretariat of SAARCFUW rotates among the National Chapters holding the Chair. Bangladesh is the current Chair.

The Fifth Council Meeting of the SAARCFUW was held in Nagpur (India) in January 2002, preceded by a seminar on the subject "Empowerment of Women in Hospitality and Tourism Industry."

SAARC Association of Town Planners

The main objective of the Association is to promote coordinated town planning in the region. Its most recent meeting was held in Colombo in March 2001. It was accorded SAARC recognition in July 1998.

At present, its Country Chapters are in Bangladesh, India, Pakistan and Sri Lanka. Its headquarters is located in Colombo.

SAARC Cardiac Society

The main objective of the Society is to foster cooperation and exchange of information in the field of cardiovascular sciences including research, training and rehabilitation programmes. It was accorded SAARC recognition in July 1998. It has Country Chapters in Bangladesh, India, Nepal, Pakistan and Sri Lanka. Its headquarters is located in Dhaka. The SAARC Cardiac Society has been meeting at least twice a year. It held its last meeting in February 2002 in New Delhi. The Society has developed several guidelines pertaining to primary and secondary prevention of coronary heart diseases.

SAARC Diploma Engineers Forum (SDEF) SDEF was recognized by SAARC in January 2002. The Forum was established with the objectives of exchanging technical information and experiences for the welfare of the Member Countries and to organize seminars, symposia, workshops, technical fairs with joint efforts by diploma engineers of the SAARC countries.

SDEF has organized a regional seminar and international conference in Dhaka on the Opportunities and Challenges of the Mid-level Technical Manpower

Development for Sustainable Economic Progress in Asia and Pacific Countries on 18-20 May 2002 in collaboration with the Colombo Plan Staff College. Its Nepal Chapter also organized a seminar on "Role of Engineering Professionals in Poverty Alleviation and Engineering Council Act" in August 2002 in Kathmandu. Its headquarter is located in Dhaka.

SAARC Teachers' Federation (STF)

STF was recognized by SAARC in January 2002. Since its recognition, STF Council has met in January and April 2002 in Kathmandu. The latter meeting was followed by a workshop which identified activities for STF and member organizations with special emphasis on the role of the teaching community in social development. Its headquarter is located in Kathmandu with a rotating Secretariat.

Foundation of SAARC Writers and Literature (FSWL)

FSWL and its affiliated Chapters have been working to foster people-to-people contacts in the region especially amongst the writers and intellectuals of South Asia. FSWL was recognized by SAARC in January 2002. Its headquarter is located in New Delhi.

Federation of State Insurance Organizations of SAARC Countries (FSIO)

FSIO is engaged in strengthening cooperation among the state sector insurers in the SAARC region and also in promoting cooperation with international organizations for the development of insurance industry. FSIO was recognized by SAARC in January 2002.

In view of the ongoing process of liberalization and privatization of insurance business in the SAARC region, FSIO has decided to expand its scope to include private insurers operating in SAARC countries in addition to state insurer organizations. Its headquarter is located in Colombo. It rotates its Chair.

Radiological Society of SAARC Countries (RSSC)

The establishment of the Radiological Society of SAARC Countries is a step forward to further the foundation of the scientific bond amongst SAARC Countries. The RSSC is geared towards the development and advancement of the radiological science among Member Countries through education and scientific research. The RSSC is expected to form a specialized group to monitor and coordinate the implementation of programmes and policies pertaining to the radiological science in the region. RSSC was recognized by SAARC in January 2002. Its headquarter is located in Colombo.

SAARC Surgical Care Society (SSCS)

SSCS is formed to promote understanding and cooperation among the Surgeons, Surgical Associations, Colleges, Societies and Organisations in the SAARC countries. The Society aims to develope and promote cooperation in all matters related to surgical practice, education and research, to interchange information and ideas about surgical interventions and to facilitate activities consonant with the SAARC Charter. The Society comprising representatives of its country chapters met in Dhaka in February 2002. The Society is also scheduled to hold its next meeting in August 2003 in Kandy, Sri Lanka. SSCS was recognized by SAARC in January 2002. Its headquarter is located in Kathmandu.

Coperation with Regional and International Organisations

The successive SAARC Summits have accorded priority to establishing contacts with regional groupings that have experience in economic and functional regional cooperation. In keeping with the above, the Association pursues collaborative efforts of mutual interest with a number of regional and international organizations with which it has finalized cooperation agreements.

EC

A Memorandum of Understanding (MoU) was signed between SAARC and European Commission (EC) on 10 July 1996 in Brussels. The MoU envisages cooperation between the two organizations on exchange of information, training programmes, technical assistance and any other areas jointly agreed to. Its primary objective is to draw upon the expertise of the European Commission in areas such as the Single European Market from which the process of regional economic cooperation within SAARC could benefit.

In pursuance of the MoU, SAARC and European Commission have identified the following areas for cooperation: facilitating access into the Single European Market; implementing the EUGSP Scheme including cumulative rules of origin; drawing on the EU experience for the SAFTA process; and evolving common standards and harmonisation with international obligations including certification, testing etc.

The EC has also recently amended its customs regulations to enable SAARC Member States to avail of the cumulative rules of origin under the Commission's GSP Scheme. In the first quarter of 2002, the project on EU's GSP scheme and implications of the EU granting the facility of regional cumulation to SAARC were exhaustively covered through a series of workshops in Member States. A User-Manual on the GSP Scheme has accordingly been prepared and uploaded in the Secretariat's website.

Dialogue between the EU and SAARC at the Ministerial level has taken place in 1998, 1999 and 2001 during the UN General Assembly Sessions.

ASEAN

Consultations between SAARC and the Association of South East Asian Nations (ASEAN) at the Ministerial level were initiated in New York in 1997 on the sidelines of the UN General Assembly Session and have since taken place in 1998, 2001 and 2002. The areas for cooperation being discussed between the two organizations include: regular consultations on UN and multilateral issues including on elective posts; sharing of expertise and experience including on poverty alleviation programmes; common approaches against terrorism; academic exchanges; programmes to combat HIV/AIDS; encouraging cooperation between ASEAN and SAARC Chambers of Commerce; encouraging people-topeople contact; and closer Secretariat-to-Secretariat consultations.

UNCTAD

A Memorandum of Understanding (MoU) on Trade Control Measures and on Trade Analysis and Information System (TRAINS) was signed between SAARC and United Nations Conference on Trade and Development (UNCTAD) in February 1993.

Under the MoU, it has been the responsibility of the SAARC Secretariat to update the UNCTAD Database on Trade Control Measures in respect of SAARC Member Countries for incorporation in the updated versions of TRAINS CD-ROM.

The TRAINS CD-ROM (Spring 2001, Version 8.0) contains trade control measures of 119 countries of the world including 44 tariff schedules for 2000 as well as 1999 import data by origin at the Harmonised System 6-digit level for 65 countries. It also includes data on trade control measures in respect of all SAARC Member Countries.

UNICEF

A Cooperation Agreement between SAARC and United Nations Children's Fund (UNICEF) was signed on 10 December 1993. It envisages cooperation in implementing SAARC decisions on children through an agreed agenda that includes preparation of joint studies, exchange of documentation and monitoring of implementation.

In pursuance of the Agreement, the SAARC Secretariat and UNICEF Regional Office for South Asia (ROSA) have been holding regular consultations to help implement SAARC directives on children including those of the Ministerial Conferences on Children of South Asia in New Delhi (1986), Colombo (1992) and Rawalpindi (1996).

In addition, the Secretariat associated itself with UNICEF sponsored Twenty-fourth Annual Session of the high-level Administrative Committee on Coordination/ Sub-Committee on Nutrition held in Kathmandu in March 1997; Regional Meeting on Ending Violence Against Women and Girls in South Asia held in Kathmandu in October 1997; "SAARC Meena Day" as part of the regional launch of Meena; Girl Child Week on 22-26 September 1998; inter-country Meeting on Polio Eradication in Kathmandu in March 2000; and the Ministerial level South Asian Preparatory Meeting for the UN Special Session on Children in Kathmandu in May 2001.

APT

The Memorandum of Understanding (MoU) signed between SAARC and Asia Pacific Telecommunity (APT) in February 1994 envisages cooperation between the two organisations to promote the growth of telecommunications in order to accelerate economic and social development in the region.

Under the MoU, SAARC and APT exchange information, publications and documents in their respective field of activities as also technical and operational details of plans for improvement of national, regional and international telecommunications networks. Collaboration between the two organizations is also intended in planning and development of networks, transfer of technology, promoting international standards, development of human resources and application of telecommunications in areas such as health, education, environment, transport and tourism.

ESCAP

A Framework Agreement for cooperation between SAARC and Economic and Social Commission for Asia and the Pacific (ESCAP) was signed in February 1994. The Agreement provides for cooperation on development issues through preparation of joint studies, holding of workshops and seminars, and exchange of information and documentation in poverty alleviation, human resources development, trade promotion, foreign direct investment, environmental protection, prevention of drug trafficking and infrastructure development. SAARC and ESCAP interact under the aegis of the Consultative Meetings of the Executive Heads of Sub-regional Organisations in Asia and the Pacific, and ESCAP. The last such meeting was held in Bali in September 2002.

UNDP

The Memorandum of Understanding (MoU) signed between SAARC and United Nations Development Programme (UNDP) in July 1995 embodies a general agreement for broad-based collaboration for promoting sustainable human development for eradicating poverty; preservation and protection of the environment; regeneration of natural resources; employment creation; enhancing the role of women in development; undertaking periodic consultation for joint activities; publishing studies on priority concerns; and exchanging relevant reports.

Cooperation between SAARC and UNDP has been particularly close in the area of poverty alleviation. UNDP carried out programmes under South Asia Poverty Alleviation Programme in specific locations in six member countries of SAARC to promote social mobilisation with a view to reducing poverty in South Asia.

SAARC and UNDP also collaborated in the organisation of the ministerial level meeting held in Kathmandu in May 2001 on South Asian Poverty Alleviation. In May 2002 the SAARC Secretariat in collaboration with the United Nations Office for Project Services (UNDP/UNOPS) organized a Workshop in Kathmandu to finalise the format of the Regional Poverty Profile (RPP). Ever since UNDP has provided assistance in the finalization of the RPP.

UNDCP

SAARC signed a Memorandum of Understanding (MoU) with United Nations Drug Control Programme (UNDCP) in August 1995 to help coordinate efforts in combating drug trafficking and drug abuse in the region. The MoU envisages mutual consultation and exchange of information between the two organisations with a view to developing and implementing joint activities on human resources development; improving regional cooperation on drug intelligence through the SAARC Drug Offences Monitoring Desk, legislation, financial investigation, money laundering, and precursor control; and the establishment of a networking arrangement among existing institutions in drug abuse prevention.

A Joint UNDCP-SAARC Workshop on Drug Trafficking and Drug Abuse was held in Colombo in 1996. This was followed by a Joint Workshop on Policy Formulation in the Area of Precursor Control held at the SAARC Secretariat in August 2001. UNDCP participated in the first meeting of the SAARC Coordination Group of Drug Law Enforcement Agencies held at the SAARC Secretariat, Kathmandu on 2-3 May 2001.

ITU

The Memorandum of Understanding (MoU) between SAARC and International Telecommunications Union (ITU) was signed in March 1997, providing a framework agreement for ensuring closer cooperation and coordination of efforts between SAARC and ITU. The areas covered by the MoU include development of telecommunications and telematic services as well as improvement of the quality of voice and non-voice telecommunications services in the region. As provided for in the MoU, SAARC and ITU jointly work towards improving the productivity and efficiency of the telecommunications organisations and networks in the region.

CIDA

A Memorandum of Cooperation between SAARC and Canadian International Development Agency (CIDA) was signed on 2 July 1997 to promote cooperation and mutually beneficial interactions in areas such as poverty eradication, economic cooperation and trade, social and human resources development, and sustainable economic growth and development.

A workshop on NAFTA/SAFTA was organised by the SAARC Secretariat in collaboration with CIDA in December 1998. The workshop facilitated the sharing of relevant experiences of the North American Free Trade Area (NAFTA) for the creation of a free trade area in South Asia.

Cooperation between CIDA and SAARC in the field of health is proceeding with the involvement of the SAARC Tuberculosis Centre in Kathmandu. The third meeting of the Joint Steering Committee for the SAARC-Canada regional TB and HIV/AIDS project was held at the Secretariat in March 2003.

WHO

SAARC and World Health Organisation (WHO) signed a Memorandum of Understanding (MoU) in August 2000 to mutually cooperate in agreed ways to help Member Countries strive towards the goal of Health for All. The MoU envisages collaboration between WHO and the SAARC Tuberculosis Centre in Kathmandu, and other institutions in South Asia, particularly those active in the field of malaria, tuberculosis, and HIV/AIDS.

Under the MoU, the two organizations promote research, analysis and dissemination of information with a view to enhancing technical cooperation and human resources development including programmes for women and children, and mobilising innovative action in favour of the underprivileged.

As part of the agreed programmes flowing from the MoU, the STC has been organising activities on cross-border issues and conducting training courses on TB, HIV, Malaria and Kalaazar.

UNIFEM

A Memorandum of Understanding (MoU) was signed between SAARC and United Nations Fund for Women (UNIFEM) on 30 December 2001 in Kathmandu. Under the MoU, SAARC and UNIFEM agree to help Member States strive towards the goals of Gender Equality based on the empowerment approach in terms of the Beijing Platform for Action (BPFA) and the Beijing Plus Five Outcome Document and encourage mutual learning and cross fertilization among developing countries for effectively tackling the challenges posed by gender discrimination and promoting women's human rights and women's participation. SAARC was represented at the Fourth South Asia Regional meeting on Commemorating Beijing organized by UNIFEM in Paro, Bhutan on 19 May 2003.

UNEP

The Third Special Session of the Standing Committee in Colombo in August 2001 authorized the Secretary-General to develop common projects with United Nations Environment Programme (UNEP) in the areas of sharing of expertise for the development of collective approaches for the protection of bio-resources and capacity building and training with a view to facilitating implementation of Multilateral Environment Agreements (MEAs).

SAARC and UNEP have since initiated consultations on evolving joint programmes in these areas. Accordingly, on the basis of the Letter of Agreement signed between SAARC and UNEP, the Third Sub-regional Workshop Towards the Effective Implementation of the Chemicals and Hazardous Wastes

Related Conventions: South Asia was held in Kathmandu from 18-20 December 2002 with participation from SAARC Member Countries. Similar activities are expected to be held in the field of bio-resources.

The Twenty-eighth Session of the Standing Committee in Kathmandu in August 2002 authorized the SAARC Secretary-General to pursue negotiations to finalize a cooperation agreement with UNEP. Pursuant to this directive, a draft MoU between the two organizations is being finalized.

SACEP

The Twenty-eighth Session of the Standing Committee in Kathmandu in August 2002 requested the Secretary-General to discuss with South Asia Cooperative Environment Programme (SACEP) suitable modalities of cooperation between the two organizations.

Accordingly, the Secretariat has since initiated discussions with SACEP in developing a cooperation agreement spelling out a broad outline of modalities of cooperation between the two organizations. A draft MoU prepared on the basis of these discussions is under consideration of SACEP.

The SAARC Secretariat

The SAARC Secretariat was established in Kathmandu on 16 January 1987. Its role is to coordinate and monitor the implementation of SAARC activities, service the meetings of the Association and serve as the channel of communication between SAARC and other international organisations. The Secretariat has also been increasingly utilised as the venue for SAARC meetings.

The Secretariat comprises the Secretary-General, seven Directors and the General Services Staff. The Secretary- General is appointed by the Council of Ministers upon nomination by a Member State on the principle of rotation in alphabetical order. The Ninth SAARC Summit (Male', May 1997) extended the tenure of the Secretary-General from two to three years.

The following have served as Secretaries-General:

— Abul Ahsan from Bangladesh (16 Jan 1987 - 15 Oct 1989);

— Kant Kishore Bhargava from India (17 Oct 1989- 31 Dec 1991);

— Ibrahim Hussain Zaki from the Maldives (1 Jan 1992- 31 Dec 1993);

— Yadab Kant Silwal from Nepal (1 Jan 1994 - 31 Dec 1995);

— Naeem U.Hasan from Pakistan (1 Jan 1996 - 31 Dec 1998); and

— Nihal Rodrigo from Sri Lanka (1 Jan 1999 - 10 Jan 2002).

The present Secretary-General, Q.A.M.A. Rahim from Bangladesh assumed office on 11 January 2002. The Directors are appointed by the Secretary-General upon nomination by Member States for a period of three years. In special circumstances, the term may be extended by the Secretary-General for a period not exceeding another full term, in consultation with the Member State concerned.

Financial Arrangement

Member States make provision in their national budgets for financing activities and programmes under the SAARC framework, including for their assessed contributions to the Secretariat budget and those of the Regional Centres. The financial provision thus made is announced annually at the meeting of the Standing Committee.

The annual budget of the Secretariat, both for capital as well as recurrent expenditure, is shared by Member States on the basis of an agreed formula.

The initial cost of the main building of the Secretariat, together with all facilities and equipment, as well as that of the annex building completed in 1993 was met by His Majesty's Government of Nepal.

In the case of SAARC Regional Centres, a minimum of forty percent of the institutional cost is borne by the respective host governments and the balance is shared by all Member States on the basis of an agreed formula. The capital expenditure of Regional Centres, which includes physical infrastructure, furnishing, machines, equipment etc. are normally borne by the respective host governments. Programme expenditure of regional institutions is also shared by Member States according to an agreed formula. Regarding approved activities in the SAARC Calendar, local expenses including hospitality are borne by the host Government while the cost of travel is met by the sending Government. For meeting these expenses, Member States make voluntary pledges every year.

2

Charter of South Asian Association for Regional Cooperation

We, the Heads of State or Government of BANGLADESH, BHUTAN, INDIA, MALDIVES, NEPAL, PAKISTAN and SRI LANKA;

1. Desirous of promoting peace, stability, amity and progress in the region through strict adherence to the principles of the UNITED NATIONS CHARTER and NON-ALIGNMENT, particularly respect for the principles of sovereign equality, territorial integrity, national independence, non-use of force and non-interference in the internal affairs of other States and peaceful settlement of all disputes;

2. Conscious that in an increasingly interdependent world, the objectives of peace, freedom, social justice and economic prosperity are best achieved in the SOUTH ASIAN region by fostering mutual understanding, good neighbourly relations and meaningful cooperation among the Member States which are bound by ties of history and culture;

3. Aware of the common problems, interests and aspirations of the peoples of SOUTH ASIA and the need for joint action and enhanced cooperation within their respective political and economic systems and cultural traditions;

4. Convinced that regional cooperation among the countries of SOUTH ASIA is mutually beneficial, desirable and necessary for promoting the welfare and improving the quality of life of the peoples of the region;

5. Convinced further that economic, social and technical cooperation among the countries of SOUTH ASIA would contribute significantly to national and collective self-reliance;

6. Recognising that increased cooperation, contacts and exchanges among the countries of the region will contribute to the promotion of friendship and understanding among their peoples;

7. Recalling the DECLARATION signed by their Foreign Ministers in NEW DELHI on August 2, 1983 and noting the progress achieved in regional cooperation;

8. Reaffirming their determination to promote such cooperation within an institutional framework;

DO HEREBY AGREE to establish an organisation to be known as SOUTH ASIAN ASSOCIATION FOR REGIONAL COOPERATION hereinafter referred to as the ASSOCIATION, with the following objectives, principles, institutional and financial arrangements:

Article I
OBJECTIVES

The objectives of the ASSOCIATION shall be:

a) to promote the welfare of the peoples of SOUTH ASIA and to improve their quality of life;

b) to accelerate economic growth, social progress and cultural development in the region and to provide all individuals the opportunity to live in dignity and to realise their full potentials;

c) to promote and strengthen collective self-reliance among the countries of SOUTH ASIA;

d) to contribute to mutual trust, understanding and appreciation of one another's problems;

e) to promote active collaboration and mutual assistance in the economic, social, cultural, technical and scientific fields;

f) to strengthen cooperation with other developing countries;

g) to strengthen cooperation among themselves in international forums on matters of common interests; and

h) to cooperate with international and regional organisations with similar aims and purposes.

Article II
PRINCIPLES

1. Cooperation within the framework of the ASSOCIATION shall be based on respect for the principles of sovereign equality, territorial integrity,

political independence, non-interference in the internal affairs of other States and mutual benefit.

2. Such cooperation shall not be a substitute for bilateral and multilateral cooperation but shall complement them.

3. Such cooperation shall not be inconsistent with bilateral and multilateral obligations.

Article III

MEETINGS OF THE HEADS OF STATE OR GOVERNMENT

The Heads of State or Government shall meet once a year or more often as and when considered necessary by the Member States.

Article IV

COUNCIL OF MINISTERS

1. A Council of Ministers consisting of the Foreign Ministers of the Member States shall be established with the following functions:

   a) formulation of the policies of the ASSOCIATION;

   b) review of the progress of cooperation under the ASSOCIATION;

   c) decision on new areas of cooperation;

   d) establishment of additional mechanism under the ASSOCIATION as deemed necessary;

   e) decision on other matters of general interest to the ASSOCIATION.

2. The Council of Ministers shall meet twice a year. Extraordinary session of the Council may be held by agreement among the Member States.

Article V
STANDING COMMITTEE

1. The Standing Committee comprising the Foreign Secretaries shall have the following functions:
   a) overall monitoring and coordination of programme of cooperation;
   b) approval of projects and programmes, and the modalities of their financing;
   c) determination of inter-sectoral priorities;
   d) mobilisation of regional and external resources;
   e) identification of new areas of cooperation based on appropriate studies.
2. The Standing Committee shall meet as often as deemed necessary.
3. The Standing Committee shall submit periodic reports to the Council of Ministers and make reference to it as and when necessary for decisions on policy matters.

Article VI
TECHNICAL COMMITTEES

1. Technical Committees comprising representatives of Member States shall be responsible for the implementation, coordination and monitoring of the programmes in their respective areas of cooperation.

2. They shall have the following terms of reference:

   a) determination of the potential and the scope of regional cooperation in agreed areas;

   b) formulation of programmes and preparation of projects;

   c) determination of financial implications of sectoral programmes;

   d) formulation of recommendations regarding apportionment of costs;

   e) implementation and coordination of sectoral programmes;

   f) monitoring of progress in implementation.

3. The Technical Committees shall submit periodic reports to the Standing Committee.

4. The Chairmanship of the Technical Committees shall normally rotate among Member States in alphabetical order every two years.

5. The Technical Committees may, inter-alia, use the following mechanisms and modalities, if and when considered necessary:

   a) meetings of heads of national technical agencies;

   b) meetings of experts in specific fields;

   c) contact amongst recognised centres of excellence in the region.

Article VII

ACTION COMMITTEES

The Standing Committee may set up Action Committees comprising Member States concerned with implementation of projects involving more than two but not all Member States.

Article VIII
SECRETARIAT

There shall be a Secretariat of the ASSOCIATION.

Article IX
FINANCIAL ARRANGEMENTS

1. The contribution of each Member State towards financing of the activities of the ASSOCIATION shall be voluntary.
2. Each Technical Committee shall make recommendations for the apportionment of costs of implementing the programmes proposed by it.
3. In case sufficient financial resources cannot be mobilised within the region for funding activities of the ASSOCIATION, external financing from appropriate sources may be mobilised with the approval of or by the Standing Committee.

Article X
GENERAL PROVISIONS

1. Decisions at all levels shall be taken on the basis of unanimity.
2. Bilateral and contentious issues shall be excluded from the deliberations.

IN FAITH WHEREOF We Have Set Our Hands And Seals Hereunto.

DONE In DHAKA, BANGLADESH, On This The Eighth Day Of December Of The Year One Thousand Nine Hundred Eighty Five.

Hussain Muhammad Ershad
PRESIDENT OF THE PEOPLE'S REPUBLIC OF BANGLADESH

Jigme Singye Wangchuk
KING OF BHUTAN

Rajiv Gandhi
PRIME MINISTER OF THE REPUBLIC OF INDIA

Maumoon Abdul Gayoom
PRESIDENT OF THE REBUPLIC OF MALDIVES

Birendra Bir Bikram Shah Dev
KING OF NEPAL

Muhammad Zia-ul-Haq
PRESIDENT OF THE ISLAMIC REPUBLIC OF PAKISTAN

Junius Richard Jayewardene
PRESIDENT OF DEMOCRATIC SOCIALIST REPUBLIC OF SRI LANKA

3

India's Relation with Neighbours

India is the world's second most populous nation (after China) and the seventh largest in area. With a land area of 32,87,263 sq km, India is about 3,000 km (1,875 mi) long and 3000 km wide and has, because of its peninsular shape, a shoreline of about 7,000 km (4,400 mi) along the Bay of Bengal on the east and the Arabian Sea on the west. The land frontier of about 5,700 km (3,600 mi) is shared with Pakistan on the west; by China (mostly Tibet), Nepal and Bhutan on the north; and by Bangladesh and Myanmar (Burma) on the east. The Indian island groups of Lakshadweep are off the western coast and the Andaman and Nicobar islands are located in the eastern portion of the Bay of Bengal.

Thus, India's geographical location endows us with vast maritime, economic and energy resources, sea-borne trade, living and non-living seabed resources and equally enormous deposits of oil and gas. However, at the same time, these geographical features also entail major security implications.

The exploration and exploitation of our resources, our maritime assets, our considerable maritime infrastructure, the long coastline in the North Indian Ocean region, our far-flung island territories and significant imports from the Gulf through this region all have complex security implications. The North Arabian Sea has always been strategically and economically very critical to India and the world, primarily due to the sizeable cargoes of oil transported from the Persian Gulf and the Red Sea to both the developed and developing nations. The importance of the North Arabian Sea is further accentuated by the concentration of oil energy assets along the Saurashtra Coast and the Gulf of Kutch.

The region accounts for four declared nuclear weapon states, a fifth undeclared but widely perceived as one, and the presence of nuclear fleets of non-Asian countries in Asian waters. Most of these states produce and export missiles, with reach sufficient to cover much of India, or in the case of China, all of it.

Militancy in different regions of India by groups actively supported from across the borders has vitiated the security environment in the country. India's major law and order concerns centre around Pakistan sponsored insurgency in Jammu and Kashmir, inter-linked and externally supported subversive activities of militant groups in North-East and the violence perpetrated by Left-wing extremist groups elsewhere.

Pakistani agencies operating from Nepal continue to launch operations against India and this included the hijacking of Indian Airlines flight IC-814 from Kathmandu by Pakistani militants in December 1999. Another dimension to the security climate in the North-East is the number of camps of ULFA and Bodo insurgents that have been set up on the borders of certain countries neighbouring India. Countries bordering this area have a common stake in uprooting terrorism and violence from the region to enable overall development and prosperity of the people.

The ISI activities in these countries which are directed against India have been taken up at various levels with the State governments concerned. They have been sensitized to the dangers of terrorist activities on their territory. We have stressed the need for prompt remedial action given the mutual inter-dependence of the countries in our region.

The increase in smuggling activities, especially of narcotics and technologically advanced small arms, accompanied by a spurt in the terrorist related activities is another area of concern. India is located in the middle of two of the world's major narcotics producing and exporting regions – North West Pakistan and Afghanistan on the one side and Myanmar on the other. The involvement of insurgent and criminal groups in the global drug trade is a major cause of concern. Instances of currency counterfeiting that have come to the fore also pose serious challenge to security.

Sino-Pakistan and Pakistan-North Korea defence co-operation, which encompass transfer of nuclear technology, assistance in the missile development programme and the transfer of conventional military equipment to Pakistan is yet another area of concern and potential instability.

Although modern technologies have contributed much for the well-being of the people, they have not yet find the ways to establishment a world free from weapons of mass destruction. The developed nations have exhibited no inclination to eliminate or even reduce their arsenals of these weapons. On the other hand, the frequency of use of military force for the resolution of political issues in the international arena has increased. Related events the world over and, in particular, in India, Russia and the Central Asian region reflect the global trend towards greater militarisation of fundamentalist forces.

While India would continue to pursue a policy that ensures peaceful co-existence of all nations and respects their sovereignty and integrity, various developments in the international and regional security environment warrant that we remain fully prepared to protect our legitimate security interests. In furtherance of India's national security objectives, we would not hesitate to take steps to deter threats to Indian interests and defeat any aggression.

India's Foriegn Relations

Within the sub-continent, India's national security interests are closely linked to her immediate neighbours namely Myanmar, Bangladesh, Bhutan, Nepal, Sri Lanka, Maldives and Pakistan. Her relations with Nepal, Bhutan, Bangladesh, Sri Lanka and Maldives are basically stable. However, there is potential for further reinforcing the relationship both in the SAARC framework and at bi-lateral levels.

India continues to progress its co-operation with Myanmar in areas such as Border Management, Control of illegal traffickings of Narcotics, and Border Trade. A security dialogue with Myanmar has been maintained. The relationship is widening into a number of developmental areas, including Agriculture, Power Generation, Transport and Science and Technology. The ISI has been trying to exploit some areas of Nepal and Bangladesh for engineering subversive activities in different parts of India, particularly the North East and J&K. This is a cause of serious concern.

Relation with Nepal

Relations between India and Nepal have been traditionally close and have reflected the links of history, culture, language and religion. These relations continued to strengthen, symbolized by exchange of high-level visits. On the auspicious occasion of the Silver jubilee of the accession to the throne of King Birendra Bir Bikram Shah Dev in 1996, the Government of India announced a Silver Jubilee Scholarship Scheme. Under this scheme, 25 Nepalese students were selected for award of scholarships for pursuing postgraduate studies in professional courses at Indian colleges/universities.

As in earlier years, India continued to play an active role in Nepal's developmental efforts. Construction of broad gauge rail links between Raxaul and Sirsa, as well as other projects, were initiated. Additional rail coaches were supplied to strengthen the service on the Jayanagar-Janakpur railway sector. Foreign Minister of Nepal visited India in December 1996 to attend the SAARC Ministerial Meeting. Letters were exchanged between the Government of India and the Government of Nepal for renewing the India-Nepal Trade Treaty for a period of five years and the Third Session of High Level Task Force was held in New Delhi on 9 August 1996. The Task Force received progress achieved in projects of Indo-Nepal cooperation.

Relation with Bhutan

India and Bhutan have traditionally enjoyed a warm and cordial relationship marked by a strong resolve to ensure welfare of people of both the countries by extensive economic cooperation. The existing friendly relationship between the two countries was further nurtured by significant exchange of views at various levels. Bilateral Plan Talks between the two countries were held from 26-30 August 1996 to review the on-going projects in Bhutan undertaken with Indian assistance during Bhutan's VII Five Year Plan (1992-97) and to discuss assistance for new projects to be taken up during Bhutan's VIII Five Year Plan (1997-2002).

Relations with Bangladesh

India's relations with Bangladesh were greatly enhanced during 1996-97. Prime Minister Sheikh Hasina paid an official visit to India from 10-12 December 1996, during which a landmark Treaty on Sharing of the Ganga Waters at Farakka was signed by the Prime Ministers of India and Bangladesh. Prime Minister Sheikh Hasina again visited India from 14-16 February 1997 to participate in the Inter-Parliamentary Specialized Conference. The Prime Minister's visit to Bangladesh on 6 and 7 January 1997 consolidated the greatly enhanced bilateral relationship between India and Bangladesh. The Fifth meeting of the India-Bangladesh Joint Economic Commission UEQ convened on 12 March 1997 agreed to step up the pace and scope of cooperation in the fields of economy and finance, trade and commerce and transport and commu-nications. Discussions with Bangladesh on security related issues yielded positive results with both sides reiterating their determination not to permit their territory to be used by insurgents and undesirable elements.

Relations with Sri Lanka

Bilateral relations with Sri Lanka continued to be close, friendly and cooperative. High level contacts were regularly maintained to strengthen bilateral cooperation in all fields of mutual interest. India has always stood for a peaceful political settlement of the ethnic issues.

During his visit to India from 19-21 June 1996, the Sri Lankan Foreign Minister briefed the Indian leadership on the security situation in Sri Lanka and also on the ongoing debate on the proposed devolution of powers to regional councils. He again came to India in December 1996 to attend the SAARC Ministerial Meeting.

The Sri Lankan President came to India on a private visit in December 1996. The Minister of External Affairs visited Sri Lanka from 19-22 January 1997 and co-chaired the third session of the Indo-Sri Lankan joint Commission. India sent 1,750 tons of rice to assist Sri Lankan efforts for rehabilitation of civilian population of Jaffna. India extended a fresh line of credit worth Rs 105 crore through an agreement signed in January 1996.

India continues to maintain very close and friendly relations with Maldives, which is an important maritime neighbor. A regular and cordial interaction was kept up during 1996-97. The Maldivies, Institute of Technical Education, a Government of India funded project, was successfully completed and the complex was handed over to the Government of Maldives on 16 September 1996.

Relations with Myanmar

India's relations with Myanmar remained cooperative and cordial. A regular and constructive interaction was maintained with Myanmar authorities in areas relevant to India's strategic interests as improved border management, border trade, security dialogue and checking traffic in narcotics and arms.

The Government of India approved the construction of Tamu-Kyigone-Kalewa and Kyigone-Kalemyo roads in Myanmar. The road would significantly improve the infrastructure in an area close to Indian borders and would provide an impetus to border trade and also improved communications.

The Myanmar Deputy Minister for Home visited India for the Fourth National Level meeting held in New Delhi in October 1996 to discuss issues such as checking illegal trade, insurgent activities and overall border management. The Fourth Indo-Myanmar meeting of Heads of Nodal Agencies under the Indo-Myartmar Agree-ment on Reducing Demanci and Preventing Illicit Trafficking in Narcotic Drugs and Psychotropic Substance was held in August 1996. Cooperation between the defense forces was discussed during the visits of Chief of Air Staff to Myanmar from 30 April-2 May 1996 and Commander-in-Chief (Air) of Myanmar to India in December 1996.

Relations with Pakistan

The Government desire to build a relationship of trust, friendship and cooperation with Pakistan. During 1996-97 the Government continued their efforts to resume the bilateral dialogue with Pakistan. The Prime Minister, in his letter of 8 June 1996 to the then Prime Minister of Pakistan, put forward the concrete proposal of resuming Foreign Secretary level talks, which had remained suspended at Pakistan's choosing since January 1994.

After the victory of the Pakistan Muslim League led by Nawaz Sharif in the February 1997 elections, the Prime Minister sent a letter to Prime Minister Nawaz Sharif reiterating India's desire to resume the bilateral dialogue as a measure to improve the relations. On receipt of a positive response from Prime Minister Nawaz Sharif, the Minister of External Affairs, in his felicitation letter to Foreign Minister of Pakitstan Gohar Ayub Khan, reiterated India's desire to convene bilateral talks at an early date.

Bilateral talks at the level of Foreign Secretaries of both the countries from 28-31 March 1997 represented official talks for the first time since January 1994. Earlier the Foreign Minister of Pakistan visited India in December 1996 to attend the SAARC Ministerial Meeting. To create a positive environment and foster people-to-people relations, the Government took several measures to increase the number of visas being issued to Pakistani nationals and to encourage increased interaction between the intellectuals, scholars, journalists and academicians of the two countries. The Government also exercised restraint in responding to the polemical statements of the Pakistani leaders. Pakistan's response to these measures was not encouraging.

Pakistan has actively encouraged terrorism against India. There is enough evidence that destabilizing India through sponsored terrorism is a matter of state policy for Pakistan. Pakistan is consciously and noticeably emerging as an epicentre of Islamic fundamentalism inducting Islamic Mujahideen into Afghanistan in the North and into Kashmir in the East. This has drawn us into a protracted Low-Intensity Conflict in Kashmir. Kashmir, however, is not the root cause for Indo-Pak tensions, but a manifestation of a deeper insecurity in that country. Embroiled as it is with internal turmoil and economic instability, these insecurities translate into a strong anti-India bias in Pakistan's perceptions.

Our policy of restraint and resolve during the Kargil crisis was appreciated by the international community. The blatant misadventure of the Pakistani military establishment in Kargil failed miserably on the politico-diplomatic and military fronts. Further, the military coup in Pakistan, which is largely a manifestation of the power struggle between the elected civilian government and the Army, with the Kargil episode as a background, is likely to have far reaching implications to the security environment in the region. Its impact is already visible in the number of suicide squads of militants operating in J&K.

Today, Pakistan's nuclear arsenal is in military hands, unfettered by even the presence of the façade of civilian-political control in a polity that has always been dominated by the military. Notwithstanding the severe economic crisis that Pakistan is currently facing, it continues to modernise its Armed Forces well beyond its legitimate requirements.

Relations with Afghanistan

India maintained her traditional policy of friendship and cooperation with Afghanistan, with the Government of

Professor Rabbani, whom it continued to support as the legitimate Government of Afghanistan. However, the situation in Afghanistan remained unstable.The situation was further exacerbated by the interference of Pakistan directly and more so through its creation, the Taliban.

With the take over of Kabul by the Taliban militia on 27 September 1996 a new dimension was added to the unstable condition in Afghanistan. The Taliban continue the pursuit of obscu-rantist doctrine and the consequent denial of human rights, especially the rights of women.

India has always supported the unity, independence, territorial integrity and sovereignty of Afghanistan. India called for the cessation of foreign interference in Afghanistan and for peaceful discussions and negotiations between Afghan parties. India also supported the efforts of the UN Secretary General and his Special Represen-tative in bringing peace to Afghanistan. India has been in the formal international peace processes on Afghanistan. India attended the Tehran conference on Afghanistan on 29 and 30 October 1996.

In recognition of India's ability to contribute to the United Nations efforts aimed at ending the crisis in Afghanistan, India was among the 19 countries invited by the UN Secretary General to a meeting in New York on 18 November 1996 of regional states and other states with influence in Afghanistan.

India was invited, despite the attempts of some countries to scuttle the invitation, to the meeting of the International Forum on Assistance to Afghanistan held on 21 and 22 January 1996 in Ashkabad, Turkmenistan.

Relation with China

India-China relations acquired maturity and substance. While continuing to address outstanding issues, including the boundary questions, both sides sought to expand mutually beneficial cooperation in all areas, particularly in the economic and technological fields. Political contacts between India and China continued through high level exchanges and consultations at other levels. President Jiang Zemin's visit to India from 28 November-1 December 1996 was part of the process of dialogue at the highest level. A significant outcome of the visit was the signing of the Agreement on Confidence Building Measures (CBMs) in the Military Field along the Line of Actual Control in the India-China Border Areas. This agreement is built on the foundation of the Agreement on the Maintenance of Peace and Tranquillity along the Line of Actual Control (LAC) in the India-China Border Areas, signed in September 1993, and provides for a number of important CBMs which will help in preserving peace and tranquillity in border areas.

The importance of paying adequate attention to each other's concerns on vital issues affecting unity, territorial integrity and security was underlined in discussions with the Chinese side during President Zemin's visit. The India-China border has been generally peaceful in recent years. Both sides have also agreed to work out details of force reduction or limitation along the LAC and put into place additional confidence building measures. Discussions on these issues were held within the framework of the India-China Joint Working Group (October 1996, Beijing) and India-China Expert Group (3-5 March 1997, New Delhi). The two countries agreed to impart a much greater economic and technological content to bilateral relations.

Relation with South-East Asia and the Pacific

During 1996-97, India's relations with the countries of the South East Asian region and the South Pacific continued to improve. As a validation of a conscious adoption of a "Look East" Policy, India became a full Dialogue Partner of the Association of South East Asian Nations (ASEAN) and participated for the first time at the Post Ministerial Conference (PMC) of ASEAN in Jakarta in July 1996. India also participated for the first time in the meeting of the ASEAN Regional Forum (ARF) which deliberates on the security and political concerns of the Asia Pacific region.

Bilateral relations with Thailand were further strengthened. Princess Dr. Chulabhorn Mahidol, the youngest daughter of the King of Thailand, visited India from 19 November-1 December 1996 in connection with the United Nations Environ-ment Program (UNEP) Award Ceremony. Another Royal guest from Thailand was the second daughter of the King, Princess Maha Chakri Sirindhorn, who visited Andaman and Nicobar Islands from 21-26 December 1996. The Festival of Thailand in India timed to coincide with 50th Anniversary of Indian independence was inaugu-rated by Princess Maha Chakri Sirindhorn. Vice-president Shri K R Narayanan transited through Bangkok on his way to Mongolia.

The Singapore government took the initiative in holding the first-ever-Global Indian Entrepreneurs Conference (GIEC) in June 1996 bringing together Indian and Indian origin businessmen from around the globe. Finance Minister Shri P Chidambaram was the keynote speaker at the Conference. India and Singapore held week long Anti Submarine Warfare Exercises off

Visakhapatnam from 3-13 March 1996. Chief of Naval Staff of Singapore participated in the concluding function of the Exercises. Bilateral trade and investment relations with Singapore continued to grow.

Malaysian Prime Minister Dr. Mahathir bin Mohamad paid a state visit to India from 19-22 December 1996 to receive the 1994 Jawaharlal Nehru Award for Interna-tional Understanding. Dr. Mahathir also delivered the First India-ASEAN Lecture instituted under the Full Dialogue Partnership with ASEAN. During the official visit of the Minister of External Affairs to Malaysia on 18 and 19 August 1996 ports, power and highways were identified as three areas where Malaysian expertise can be beneficial to India.

The Second Meeting of the Indo-Brunei joint Committee was held. Though bilateral trade between the two countries is limited, the two countries are seeking ways to expand it.

President of Philippines Fidel V Ramos paid a State visit to India from 3-5 March 1997. He was accompanied by leaders of the business community in Philippines. To further acquaint Philippines' commerce and industry with reforms in India, the Indian Embassy organized two Business Seminars on the emerging opportunities in India in the new economic environment. The second Meeting of the India-Philippines Joint Business Council was held in New Delhi in September 1996.

India continued to have friendly and close relations with Indonesia. Minister of External Affairs visited Indonesia in July 1996 to attend the ASEAN Regional Forum (ARF) and ASEAN-PMC meetings in Jakarta where India was formally admitted as member of the ARF and Full Dialogue Partner of ASEAN. Chief of

Naval Staff attended the inauguration of the Indonesia Air Show held in Jakarta on 20 June 1996. During the World Food Summit held in Rome, Prime Minister had a meeting with the Indonesian President on 16 November 1996. The two leaders discussed means to build and expand bilateral relations and the need to strengthen India's relations with ASEAN countries in general.

Indonesia agreed to India's proposal for setting up a Telemetry Tracking ground station at Biak (Kalimantan) for continuous monitoring of the Indian Space Research Organization's (ISRO) Geosynchronous Satellite Launch Vehicle (GSLV). An agreement for cooperation in the field of space science is in the final stages of negotiation. In December 1996, India and Indonesia signed a Cultural Exchange Program for the year 1997-1999 under the aegis of the India-Indonesia Cultural Agreement with a view to promoting further understanding and closer cooperation in the field of culture and education. The holding of an exclusive Indian Trade Exhibition in Jakarta in March 1996 coincided with the meeting of the Joint Business Council. FICCI opened an office in Jakarta.

India maintained very close and friendly relations with Vietnam. Prime Minister of Vietnam paid an official visit to India in March 1997. The Third Meeting of the India-Vietnam Joint Working Group (JWG) was held in New Delhi on 16 and 17 January 1997 to review progress on various bilateral cooperation programs and a Work Plan for Agricultural Cooperation was signed during the JWG meeting. Chief of Naval Staff visited Vietnam in May 1996. Another Rupee credit of Rs 90 crore on soft terms was extended to Vietnam for capital goods imports from India.

India continued to have very close and warm relations with Laos. An MOU for cooperation in the field of agriculture was negotiated. Government of India pledged to provide medicines worth Rs 15 lakh to Laos as flood relief.

Relations with Cambodia remained very friendly and warm. An agreement to set up an India-Cambodia Joint Commission on Trade, Economic, Scientific and Technological Cooperation was finalized. First Prime Minister of Cambodia Prince Norodom Ranariddh visited Bodh Gaya, Patna on 16 December 1996 on a pilgrimage.

Relations between India and Australia continued to grow in diverse fields. Australian Foreign Minister visited India from 19-23 October 1996 to launch the Australia-India New Horizons Promotion to raise Australia's profile in India. The other prominent Australian leaders who visited India to participate in the New Horizons Program during the core period of the program (22 October-8 Novem-ber 1996) were Deputy Prime Minister and Minister for Trade, Minister for Employ-ment, Education, Training and Youth Affairs, Minister for Communications and Arts, Minister for Resources and Energy and three Deputy Premiers from Tasmania, New South Wales and Western Australia and the Leader of Opposition in the Australian House of Representatives and Shadow Foreign Minister. From the Indian side Minister for Steel and Mines, Minister of Railways and Minister for Textiles visited Australia.

India-New Zealand relations continued to be friendly and cordial. Minister for Textiles visited New Zealand to inaugurate the Buyer-Seller-Meet (BSM) organized by Apparels Export Promotion Council in Auckland and to attend a meeting of the India--New

Zealand joint Business Council on Wool in Wellington. Chief of Naval Staff paid a four-day goodwill visit to New Zealand.

India opened a resident Mission in Port Moresby, Papua New Guinea (PNG), on 12 April 1996 and the first resident High Commissioner to PNG presented his credentials on 14 May 1996. Government of India established diplomatic relations with Micronesia on 29 November 1996 and also decided to establish diplomatic relations with Marshal Islands. Efforts were made to strengthen and maintain India's friendly relations with other Pacific Island countries.

Government of India closely followed developments in Fiji as well as the process of constitutional reforms, which has been set in motion. The Government expressed the hope that the implementation of the Constitution Review Commission's recommendations would be done in a manner that meets the expectations of the Fijians of Indian origin. Government of India has consistently taken the stand that the 1990 racially biased constitution should be reviewed to arrive at a constitutional arrangement that is, democratic, just, non-discriminatory and acceptable to all the communities living in Fiji.

Relation with West Asia

The West Asian and North African regions represent part of India's extended neighbourhood. India enjoys multifaceted relations with the countries of the region. This region will remain the primary source of India's energy needs for the foreseeable future. It would also continue to host a substantial Indian community that contributes to the economic well being of the region.

India also remains interested in the progress of the peace process in the Middle East. The growing links between these regions and other parts of the world in the area of ballistic missiles proliferation as well as the infusion of high technology weapon systems, have a bearing on regional security. Strategically, the Iraq-US/UN stand off has the potential to erupt into intra-regional tensions and re-induction of hi-tech weapons into the region.

Relation with Central Asia

India has historical and cultural links with Central Asia. It has always recognised the unique identity of the countries anxes of the region and was among the first to recognise their independence. For geo-political and geo-economic reasons, Central Asia attracts a large measure of external attention. Big power rivalries over their rich economic resources, especially hydrocarbons; the perennial flash point of Afghanistan, the volatility of the Tajik situation; religious fundamentalism, cross-border terrorism and arms and drugs trafficking underline the complexities of the security situation in Central Asia.

Central Asian countries and India have a common stake in countering religious extremism and terrorism. India's traditional links with the region are being strengthened through enhanced dialogue and interaction as well as India's positive and constructive participation in regional security initiatives such as the Conference on Interaction and Confidence Building in Asia (CICA). A large number of visits, including at the highest level, have been exchanged.

India has been making its contribution to the development of the region by promoting trade and investments, including through bilateral credits, and offering training facilities. In 1997 India, Iran and Turkmenistan signed a trilateral transit agreement to facilitate trade with Central Asia. India and the countries of the Central Asia have a common stake in peace and stability in the region.

Relation with Russia

With the maturing of Russian democracy, the Russian economy has started showing some signs of improvement. A resurgent Russia will gradually endeavour to assert itself in its erstwhile traditional areas of influence in keeping with its vast geographic spread, its great pool of human talent and its enormous resource base. Its recent rapprochement with China has global security dimensions.

India and the Russian Federation have longstanding mutually beneficial relations in the field of defence within the overall framework of their time-tested ties which are characterized by continuity, trust and mutual understanding. Long Term Indo-Russian Programme of Military-Technical Cooperation up to 2010 signed in December 1998 was yet another important step in this direction.

India and Russia are determined to raise the level of their multifaceted cooperation to a strategic partnership. Both countries seek a multi-polar world and share an identity of views on a wide range of issues, including on the growing scourge of international terrorism. Both appreciate the need for both bilateral and multilateral endeavours to eradicate this scourge.

Relation with USA

Based on mutual respect, mutual benefit, equality and understanding, Indo-US co-operation has improved in the recent past. High level contacts between military officials of the two countries are now increasing and the sanctions imposed by USA after May 1998 have also been lifted to an extent. The US has also resumed its IMET programme. In keeping with the improving relations between the two countries, the institutional framework including the Defence Policy Group, the Joint Technical Group and Service-to-Service level Steering Groups for co-operation evolved over the years, need to be revived and strengthened. The forthright and positive stand taken by the USA regarding Pakistan's intrusion in Kargil highlights the changing contours of Indo-US co-operation. The two countries are also engaged in discussions to assess the threat of international terrorism and measures to counter it.

India's Foreign Policy

The foundations of India's foreign policy were laid during the freedom movement when the leaders, even when fighting for independence, were engaged with the great causes of the time. The principles of India's foreign policy, that emerged then, have stood the test of time: a belief in friendly relations with all countries of the world, the resolution of conflicts by peaceful means, the sovereign equality of all states, independence of thought and action as manifested in the principles of Non-alignment, and equity in the conduct of international relations.

Under the leadership of Jawaharlal Nehru, India was the founder member of the Non-aligned Movement. India has played an active role in strengthening the Movement and making it an effective voice in representing the collective aspirations and interests o the developing countries on such vital issues as development, peace and stability. India hosted the 7th NAM Summit in New Delhi in 1983. In recent years, after the end of the Cold War, the country's foreign policy has been focused on strengthening the Movement by redefining its priorities in keeping with the changing times.

India has also been in the forefront of the world community in the struggle against colonialism. Indeed, the Independence of India itself played the role of a catalyst in removing the vestiges of colonialism in other parts of the developing world, particularly in Africa. India was also the first country to raise the question of racial discrimination in South Africa in 1946. It was at India's initiative that the AFRICA (Action for Resistance to Invasion, Colonialism and Apartheid) Fund was set up at the 8th NAM Summit in Harare in 1986. India was the Chairman of the AFRICA Fund Committee, which wound up in 1993.

A notable feature of Indian foreign policy has been its strong advocacy of general and complete disarmament, with nuclear disarmament being accorded the highest priority. Towards this end, India has taken several initiatives within the United Nations and outside. In 1988, India presented to the 3rd Session of the UN General Assembly devoted to Disarmament an Action Plan for Ushering in a Nuclear Weapons Free and Non-Violent World Order. In order to highlight international concern about the unprecedented nuclear arms race, India was also a member of the Six-Nation Five-

Continent joint Initiative in the 1980s. But while India has, and will, remain committed to nuclear disarmament, to be achieved in a time-bound framework, it has consistently and in a principled manner opposed such discriminatory treaties as the Nuclear non-Proliferation Treaty (NPT) and Comprehensive Nuclear Test Ban Treaty (CTBT) and has refused to give up its nuclear options until all countries in the world including nuclear weapon states embrace the idea of nuclear disarmament in a phased manner.

As a founder member of the United Nations, India has been firmly committed to the purposes and principles of the United Nations and has made significant contributions to its various activities, including peace-keeping operations. India has been a participant in all its peace-keeping operations including those in Korea, Egypt and Congo in earlier years and in Somalia, Angola and Rwanda in recent years. India has also played an active role in the deliberations of the United Nations on the creation of a more equitable international economic order. It has been an active member of the Group of 77, and later the core group of the G-15 nations. Other issues, such as environmentally sustainable development and the promotion and protection of human rights, have also been an important focus of India's foreign policy in international forums.

Commensurate with national interests and security, the improvement of bilateral relations is an important component of any foreign policy, and India has succeeded in establishing a network of mutually beneficial relations with all countries of the world.

The improvement of relations with its neighbours has always been one of the pillars of India's foreign policy. India played an historic and unique role in the liberation of Bangladesh which emerged as a sovereign nation in 1971. Through the implementation of the 1964 and 1974 Agreements, the issues of the stateless people of Indian origin in Sri Lanka were resolved. In 1988, India helped preserve the integrity of Maldives by coming to the assistance of that country and preventing an attempted take over by armed mercenaries.

The Indian government has taken recent initiatives to further strengthen ties with its neighbors, which have won international appreciation. These initiatives are based on five clear principles: First, with neighbors like Bangladesh, Bhutan, Maldives, Nepal and Sri Lanka, India does not ask for reciprocity but gives all that it can in good faith and trust. Secondly, no South Asian country should allow its territory to be used against the interests of another country of the region. Thirdly, none will interfere in the internal affairs of another. Fourthly, all South Asian countries must respect each other's territorial integrity and sovereignty. And finally, they should settle all their disputes through peaceful bilateral negotiations.

These tenets have paid rich dividends. A landmark Treaty has been signed with Bangladesh on the sharing of waters of the Ganga. With Bhutan and Nepal, major projects of economic collaboration have been advanced. India's relations with Sri Lanka have shown steady improvement. With Pakistan, India has consistently pursued a policy seeking to improve relations under the framework of the Simla Agreement signed in 1972 which provided for the resolution of outstanding issues peacefully and bilaterally and for establishing durable peace in the Sub-continent. Bilateral discussions with Pakistan have resumed recently and India would continue efforts to have good neighborly relations with Pakistan.

An important achievement of India's foreign policy has been the strengthening of regional co-operation. India is an active member of the South Asian Association for Regional Cooperation (SAARC) which was launched in December 1985. With India's full support, SAARC has recently taken significant steps in accelerating the pace of economic co-operation. The South Asian Preferential Trade Arrangement (SAPTA) became operational in December 1995.

At the 9th SAARC Summit in Male in May 1997, which was chaired by India, a historical decision has also been taken to strive for a South Asian Free Trade Area (SAFTA) latest by the year 2001 AD. The emergence of the Indian Ocean Rim Association for Regional Co-operation (IOR-ARC) in March 1997, as a major instrument of cooperation in the larger region, has also had the active support of India.

India's foreign policy has always regarded the concept of neighborhood as one of widening concentric circles, around a central axis of historical and cultural commonalties. From this point of view, it has always given due priority to the development of relations with South East Asia.

In 1947, India organized the Asian Relations Conference. It chaired the International Control Commission in 1954 and was a major player in the organization of the Bandung Conference in 1955. Today, India is implementing a 'Look East' policy which is underpinned by important economic considerations. Some significant steps in the pursuance of this policy have been taken with the admission of India as a full dialogue partner of ASEAN and a member of the ASEAN Regional Forum, in 1996.

An attribute of a dynamic foreign policy is the ability to respond to changing developments. The emergence of the Central Asian Republics in the aftermath of the break up of the Soviet Union was one such recent development, and India, given the strategic and economic importance of this region, has been quick to strengthen its bilateral relations with each of these Republics.

The shift in recent years by the countries of Central and East Europe to political pluralism and market-oriented structures has also seen India trying to build upon existing business and institutional linkages so as to further strengthen the traditional ties of friendship with the countries of the region.

The countries of the Gulf have a political and strategic importance for India. The region is a major market for Indian exports. Three million Indians are employed in these countries. The strengthening of ties with the region, therefore, has been a priority of India's foreign policy.

With China the aim of Indian foreign policy has been of developing a relationship of friendship, cooperation and good neighborliness, exploiting the potential for favorable growth wherever it exists, even as we seek to find a fair, reasonable and mutually acceptable solution to the outstanding border issue. Towards this aim, a series of high level visits have been exchanged, bilateral trade and economic cooperation is growing, and an Agreement on Confidence Building Measures, as part of a wider dialogue on security, has been signed.

Foreign Policy in the Changing World Order

The evolution of foreign policy that took place immediately after independence was informed with the same degree of idealism that permeated the freedom struggle. In fact, you will find that not only in the case of India, but all over the world there has been a conflict between idealism and realism in the formulation and implementation of all policies, especially foreign policy. So initially when India achieved its independence, this idealism formed the bedrock of her foreign policy and there was no dearth of issues for her to espouse. For example, the war against colonialism had started in India. In that war, the first victory was that of India. It was therefore natural for India to assume a leadership role against colonialism. It was also India's destiny to lead the fight against racism, particularly the policy of apartheid which was being practiced in South Africa. The war against colonialism and the war against racism formed, some of the basic ingredients of India's early foreign policy.

India also looked at the world and saw more and more countries achieving their freedom from colonial rule. When these newly emerging countries looked at the world, they found a world divided between the communist bloc and the non-communist bloc. It was the age of the Cold War. Under the leadership of Pandit Nehru, President Nasser and President Tito, this community of nations evolved what is known as the Non-Aligned Movement. Over a period of time, NAM not only acquired a political dimension but also strong economic content. The Group of 77 which consisted mostly of the non-aligned countries became an important instrument of negotiation and articulation of views of the developing countries in all fora where economic issues were discussed.

Immediately after the independence of India, Pt. Nehru observed "the objectives of our foreign policy are the preservation of world peace and the enlargement of human freedom". He also described the idealism of today as the realism of tomorrow. So, these were the origins of India's foreign policy and during the decade of 50s and 60s, you will notice that as a result of this idealism, India was among the most prominent countries which had not only achieved independence but was also working for the independence of other countries.

India has, and because of nonalignment, had a role in international affairs which was perhaps disproportionate to its military and economic strength. What sustained that role was the idealism and morality that informed its foreign policy. It is this idealism which gave India the stature internationally.

A broad overview suggests that when Mrs. Indira Gandhi became the Prime Minister of India, she leaned more on the realist aspects of India's foreign policy. She did not depend on idealism entirely. During her regime, a lot of things happened which clearly brought India onto the world map. India had the nuclear tests in 1974. The country went into space and the first satellite was launched in July 1980. It started to reform its economy. Clearly a change was noticeable, both in the economic content of foreign policy as well as the military and defence content. It was not that Mrs. Gandhi did not play a role internationally. She attended a number of important international meetings during her tenure as Prime Minister and hosted a number of important meetings in India. During her era, there was emphasis on disarmament, development and on the environment in the international field. These are three things that she brought into sharper focus as part of her foreign policy.

This realism was followed by subsequent regimes and the culmination of this realism was in May 1998 when India decided overtly to go for nuclear tests. India declared to the world that it was a nuclear-weapon power. In the meanwhile, in the decade of 90s a uni-polar world emerged with the collapse of the Soviet Union.

The international backdrop also underwent a dramatic change. India has launched itselves on a definite path of economic reforms, liberalization and greater integration with the global economy. During this phase, globalisation became a force which no country could ignore. Today's foreign policy is therefore more realistic based on the recognition that India's place in the comity of nations will be determined by the economic and military strength that is there to back it up. It does not mean abandonment of idealism but clearly idealism alone cannot suffice.

The guiding principle of foreign policy today is realism and the pursuit of national interest. Clearly, uni-polarism as against multi-polarism is a real issue which every country in the world has to reckon with. India is not in favour of uni-polarity and therefore the kind of world order which it envisage and are working for is not one merely of technical equality in the United Nations but greater balance among nations of the world. It should not be one country's will which alone prevails in all situations. The other impact of multi-polarity would be in the security area and in all the arrangements internationally which govern nuclear weapons, missiles, high technology, etc. India has been consistently of the view that you cannot have two categories of countries in the world – one, which has stolen technological lead over others and others who came in late. That has been the basic objection to the NPT and the Comprehensive Test Ban Treaty.

India is committed entirely and whole heartedly to disarmament. But it want every country in the world to disarm. India is also supportive of making a distinction between a responsible State and an irresponsible State. There are some States which are clearly helping other countries in nuclear proliferation. India cannot be accused of that.

The other aspect of India's foreign policy currently and for some time to come, is the phenomenon of regionalism. In order to establish a multi-polar world, smaller countries in the world are getting together and evolving themselves not merely into economic groups but also acquiring a political personality. The European Union is a good example of a group which started as a union or a conglomerate of countries for economic and trade matters but has now acquired a clear political dimension. While one must admit that EU has not been able to evolve a common position on all issues which are of political importance, EU is gradually evolving a political personality of its own. When EU can have a convergence of views on economic, political and strategic matters which are globally important, EU will perhaps be a counter balance and force in the international global situation.

India has evolved a policy to deal with regional groups such as ASEAN, CARICOM, and MERCOSUR. A few years ago, the country had its first Summit with European Union and the third summit was held recently in Copenhagen. It also had summit with ASEAN in Cambodia recently. The country is trying to forge relations with the Latin American groups and with the African groups. It will be India's policy to promote a strong regional cooperative group in South Asia and to promote friendly relations with all groups of countries which have organized themselves regionally. In this effort, economic diplomacy will be the country's principal tool.

The thrust of India's economic diplomacy in the coming days will be to work out a road map which, within a fixed time frame, will ultimately lead to a free-trade arrangement with all regional groups of developing countries. India is working on one with ASEAN and we will look at other groupings of developing countries also. It started with preferential trade arrangements and ultimately move to a free-trade arrangement.

There are today large number of Indians in information technology and other fields who are making investments in the European Union. There are technologies which India can transfer to other countries given its strength in knowledge industry. It is being increasingly recognised that India has excellent technology. With this respect which India commands, it should be possible for the country to be of greater help for the developing world and stand shoulder-to-shoulder with the developed world.

Today, the international economic order is highly skewed in favour of developed countries. This is something which has to be set right. It is difficult to pursue enlightened approaches to development in a world where overseas development assistance levels are falling, protectionism is on the rise, terms of trade are stacked in favour of the rich, debt burdens have spiralled, corporate governance needs urgent redefinition and the volatility of international capital transfers has affected productive investment flows to the South.

It is depressing to note the statistics given in the Human Development Report 2002 that 2.8 billion people still live on less than US$ 2 a day and the richest 1% of the world's people receive as much income each year as the poorest 57%. Industrial country tariffs on imports from developing countries are four times those on imports from other industrial countries. In addition, as is well known, OECD countries provide US$ 1 billion a day on domestic agricultural subsidies which is more than six times what they spend on ODA for developing countries. These figures bring out the enormity of the inequity which exists in the world today.

India will continue to coordinate activities with other developing countries in order to be able to deal with this problem and create an environment which is more equitable. Economic development will continue to be a primary concern of India's foreign policy. India has supported the millennium goals of the United Nations.

Conflict, as is well known, has acquired a new dimension because non-State actors have got into the act of creating new trans-national conflicts which did not exist before. It is easier to deal with State actors and negotiate with them. It is very difficult to deal with shadowy figures who are always in the background. The kind of terror India faced recently tells its own tale. The country has been at the receiving end of cross-border terrorism for almost two decades.

The world was not prepared to take as much notice of it as it should have. But, the entire outlook underwent a sea-change after 9/11. Today, the world have an international coalition against terrorism, arrangements in place to freeze terrorist financing, Security Council Resolution 1373, etc. Now the world has veered around to the formulation that terrorism in all its forms and all its manifestations is bad and cannot be tolerated. But, there is still a disconnect between the kind of instruments that are prepared to use for dealing with terrorism and terrorists.

India have a certain amount of disappointment with the international community because of the soft attitude they have adopted towards its neighbour which is exporting terrorism into India. As long as this continues, one will be compelled to say that the world has not yet arrived at a single standard. There is still a double standard in dealing with terrorism.

In recent years, the nuclear tests which India carried out in May 1998 was a watershed. The world did not look at it kindly and the country was subjected to economic sanctions. India has emerged today as a key global player. This change which has come about within four-and-a-half years from the nuclear tests is remarkable in itself and calls for a much deeper study of Indian diplomacy during this period. Moreover, India is a legitimate aspirant for a permanent seat in the Security Council of the UN and there are by now a number of countries which have publicly pledged their support. One important strength apart from IT and knowledge industry which India has acquired over the last decade or so, is the emergence of the Indian diaspora and the political influence they enjoy in various countries, be it the EU, the US or elsewhere. The Indian diaspora has an important economic role to play in the development of India.

4

Declaration of the First SAARC Summit, Dhaka

The Dhaka Declaration of the Heads of State or Government of the Member Countries of South Asian Association for Regional Cooperation issued on 8th December 1985.

Introduction

1. The President of Bangladesh, the King of Bhutan, the Prime Minister of India, the President of Maldives, the King of Nepal, the President of Pakistan and the President of Sri Lanka met in Dhaka on 7 and 8 December 1985.
2. The Heads of State or Government underscored the historic significance of their first ever South Asian Summit meeting. They considered it to be a tangible manifestation of their determination to cooperate regionally, to work together towards finding solutions towards their common problems in a spirit of friendship, trust and mutual understanding and to the creation of an order based on mutual respect, equity and shared benefits.

3. They recognized that periodic meetings at their level were central to the promotion of mutual trust, confidence and cooperation among their countries.

4. The Heads of State or Government reaffirmed that their fundamental goal was to accelerate the process of economic and social development in their respective countries through the optimum utilization of their human and material resources, so as to promote the welfare and prosperity of their peoples and to improve their quality of life. They were conscious that peace and security was an essential prerequisite for the realization of this objective.

5. The leaders of the South Asian countries reaffirmed their commitment to the UN Charter and the principles governing sovereign equality of States, peaceful settlement of disputes, non-interference in internal affairs and non-use or threat of use of force against the territorial integrity and political independence of other States. They reiterated that the United Nations constituted the most important forum for the resolution of all issues affecting international peace and security.

6. They also reaffirmed their deep conviction in the continuing validity and relevance of the objectives of the Nonaligned movement as an important force in international relations.

7. The Heads of State or Government acknowledged that the countries of South Asia, who constituted one-fifth of humanity, were faced with the formidable challenges posed by poverty, underdevelopment, low levels of production, unemployment and pressure of population compounded by exploitation of the past and other

adverse legacies. They felt that, bound as their countries were by many common values rooted in their social, ethnic, cultural and historical traditions, regional cooperation provided a logical response to these problems. They were conscious of their individual and regional strengths, their potential as a huge market, their substantial human and natural resources and the complementarities of their economies. They were confident that with effective regional cooperation, they could make optimum use of these capacities for the benefit of their peoples, accelerate the pace of their economic development and enhance their national and collective self-reliance. They were convinced that their countries, which had made important contributions to the enrichment of human civilization, could together play their due role in international relations and influence decisions which affected them.

8. The Heads of State or Government emphasised that strengthening of regional cooperation in South Asia required greater involvement of their peoples. They agreed to increase interaction and further promote people-to-people contacts at various levels among their countries. To this end, they decided to take steps to create awareness and public opinion in the region.

9. The Heads of State or Government welcomed the progress already made in the implementation of the Integrated Programme of Action in the nine mutually agreed areas. They expressed their desire to consolidate and further expand cooperative efforts within an appropriate institutional frame work in a spirit of partnership and equality.

10. The leaders were convinced that they could effectively pursue their individual and collective objectives and improve the quality of life of their peoples only in an atmosphere of peace and security. In this context, they expressed concern at the deteriorating international political situation. They were alarmed at the unprecedented escalation of arms race particularly in its nuclear aspect. They recognized that mankind today was confronted with the threat of self extinction arising from a massive accumulation of the most destructive weapons ever produced. The arms race intensified international tension and violated the principles of the UN Charter. The leaders called upon the nuclear weapons-states for urgent negotiations for a comprehensive Test Ban Treaty leading to the complete cessation of testing, production and deployment of nuclear weapons. In this connection, they welcomed the recent meeting between President Reagan and General Secretary Gorbachev in Geneva and expressed the hope that the meeting would have a positive effect on international peace and security.

11. The Heads of State or Government expressed deep concern at the continuing crises in the global economy. They underscored that deteriorating economic and social conditions had seriously retarded developing countries. Sharply falling commodity prices, deterioration in the terms of trade, intensification of protectionist measures, spiralling debt burden and a decline in the flow of external resources, especially concessional assistance, had caused a serious setback to the economic development of the developing countries. These had been compounded by natural disasters and

precarious world food security situation affecting developing countries. They also expressed concern over the diminishing capacity of international financial and technical institutions to respond effectively to the needs of the disadvantaged and poorer countries and regretted that the spirit of multilateral cooperation had begun to falter and weaken. This was particularly disturbing in the face of increased interdependence of developed and developing countries and the fact that economic revival of North was closely linked to economic progress in South. They believed that developments during the past decades had clearly demonstrated the structural imbalances and inequities inherent in the existing international economic system and its inadequacy to deal with problems of development.

12. They strongly urged that determined efforts should be made by the international community towards realization of the goals and targets of the International Development Strategy as well as the Substantial New Programme of Action for the Least Developed Countries. They called for urgent resumption of the North-South dialogue and early convening of an International Conference on Money and Finance for Development with universal participation.

13. The Heads of State or Government were conscious of the historic importance of the Dhaka Summit and reiterated their conviction that the launching of the South Asian Association for Regional Cooperation (SAARC), which they had established at this meeting, would place regional cooperation on a firm foundation, play an important role in accelerating the pace of economic and social development of their

countries, promote the objectives of individual and collective self reliance and further the cause of peace, progress and stability in their region and the world.

14. The Heads of State or Government of Bhutan, India, Maldives, Nepal, Pakistan and Sri Lanka were deeply appreciative of the exemplary Chairmanship of their Meeting by the President of Bangladesh. They expressed their profound gratitude for the warm and gracious hospitality extended to them by the Government and the people of Bangladesh and for the excellent arrangements made for the meeting.

****

Joint Press Release

Joint Press Release Issued at the Conclusion of the First SAARC Summit in Dhaka on 7-8 December 1985 The President of Bangladesh, the King of Bhutan, the Prime Minister of India, the President of Maldives, the King of Nepal, the President of Pakistan and the President of Sri Lanka met in Dhaka on 7 and 8 December, 1985.

The Heads of State or Government signed a Charter of the South Asian Association for Regional Cooperation on the 8th of December, 1985. They also adopted the Dhaka Declaration. They approved that the Standing Committee should set up a Study Group to examine the problem of terrorism a it affects the security and stability of Member States of SAARC. They further directed the Council of Ministers to consider the report of this Study Group and submit recommendations to them as to how best the Member States could cooperate among themselves to solve this. They also approved that a similar exercise be carried out with regard to the problem of drug trafficking and abuse. They decided that the Member Governments should concert their views on the ongoing discussions on New International Economic Order and the improvement of the World Trading System through GATT taking particularly into account the interest of the least developed among the developing countries. For this purpose it was decided to convene a Ministerial level meeting. The Standing Committee should convene a meeting to prepare for it. The Heads of State or Government gratefully accepted the offer of the President of Pakistan to host both these meetings. The Heads of State or Government emphasized that women should increasingly participate in activities at the regional level within the framework of SAARC and that Programmes and Projects should be devised to ensure their active participation in the development process. They therefore directed the Standing Committee to convene a Ministerial Level Conference on the subject to identify the areas of activities and plan a Programme of Action. They gratefully accepted the offer of the Prime Minister of India to host such a conference. The Heads of State or Government who have decided that the Association shall have a Secretariat directed the Foreign Ministers to consider details regarding its location, structure, functions and financing and submit those for the consideration of Heads of State or Government. The Heads of State or Government decided to hold their next meeting in November, 1986. They gratefully accepted the offer of the Prime Minister of India to host that meeting. They also gratefully accepted the offer of the King of Bhutan to host the Annual SAARC Summit of 1987. The Heads of State or Government unanimously accepted the recommendation of the Fourth Meeting of Foreign Ministers on the emblem of SAARC.

5

Declaration of the Second SAARC Summit, Bangalore

The Bangalore Declaration of the Heads of State or Government of the member countries of the South Asian Association for Regional Cooperation issued on November 17, 1986.

Introduction

1. The President of Bangladesh, the King of Bhutan, the Prime Minister of India, the President of Maldives, the King of Nepal, the Prime Minister of Pakistan and the President of Sri Lanka assembled at the second SAARC Summit in Bangalore on 16 and 17 November, 1986.
2. The Heads of State or Government reiterated their desire of promoting peace, stability, amity and progress in the region through strict adherence to the principles of the United Nations Charter and Non-alignment, particularly respect for the principles of

sovereign equality, territorial integrity, national independence, non-use of force and non-interference in the internal affairs of other States and peaceful settlement of disputes.

3. The Heads of State or Government reaffirmed the will of their peoples and Governments to work together in accordance with the SAARC Charter to devise common policies and approaches for finding common solutions to the shared problems that all of them face. They stressed that mutual trust, goodwill and understanding must animate their cooperative effort under SAARC. Progress and prosperity in each country would redound to the benefit of others. This was what constituted the SAARC spirit.

4. The leaders reaffirmed that the principal goal of SAARC was to promote the welfare of the peoples of South Asia, to improve their quality of life, to accelerate economic growth, social programmes and cultural development in the region and to provide all individuals the opportunity to live in dignity and to realize their full potential.

5. The Heads of State or Government recalled that the countries of South Asia had been linked by age-old cultural, social and historical traditions. These had led to enriching interaction of ideas, values, culture and philosophies. These commonalities constituted solid foundations for regional cooperation for addressing more effectively the economic and social problems.

6. The Heads of State or Government recalled that the South Asian Association for Regional Cooperation was the most populous regional grouping in the world. The countries of the region had large, rich and

varied human and natural resources. They expressed their determination to achieve the optimum utilization of these resources by intensifying their cooperation, bearing in mind the immense present and potential complementarities among their economies. They recognised that this would require increasing exchange among their countries, on the basis of mutual benefit, of ideas, experience and technology as well as goods and services, which utilize and enhance the productive capacity of each of their countries and build their collective self reliance. They were convinced that the countries of South Asia which had been the cradle of human civilization and culture could, acting together co-operatively and cohesively, once again play their due role in the comity of nations.

7. The Heads of State or Government reiterated the great importance of the increasing involvement of the people for ensuring the success of regional co-operation. They emphasized the need for promoting greater contacts among the peoples of the region through such action as regular and frequent interchange of scholars, academics, artists, authors, professionals and businessmen as well as facilitation of tourism

8. The Heads of State or Government noted with satisfaction that considerable progress had been achieved in the implementation of SAARC Integrated Programme of Action. They expressed their firm commitment to consolidate and streamline further the implementation of the IPA. They agreed that a progressive movement towards more concrete and action-oriented projects and programmes was

essential to ensure more tangible benefits from SAARC to the peoples of the region. The Heads of State or Government emphasized the importance of expanding cooperative endeavours under SAARC. They welcomed the establishment of the Technical Committees on Women in Development, and on the Prevention of Drug Trafficking and Drug Abuse.

9. The Heads of State or Government welcomed the signing of the Memorandum of Understanding on the establishment of the SAARC Secretariat by the Council of Ministers and their decision to locate the Secretariat in Kathmandu and appoint Ambassador Abul Ahsan of Bangladesh as the first Secretary-General of SAARC. They were convinced that the establishment of the Secretariat would assist in the coordination of SAARC activities and more fruitful implementation of its programmes and projects.

10. The Heads of State or Government recognised that meeting the needs of all children was the principal means of human resources development. Children should, therefore, be given the highest priority in national development planning. The Heads of State or Government underlined the importance of enhancing public consciousness and building a national political consensus on the rights of the children. In this context they called for an early conclusion and adoption of the UN Convention on the Rights of the Child. They subscribed to the goals of universal immunization by 1990, universal primary education, maternal and child nutrition, provision of safe drinking water and adequate shelter before 2000 A. D. They also believed that it should be possible to ensure at the end of the century, that no child need

die or be denied development, for reasons of material poverty in the family. They directed the Standing Committee to undertake annual reviews of the situation of children in the SAARC countries, monitoring of programmes and exchange of experience.

11. The Heads of State or Government agreed that co-operation among SAARC States was vital if terrorism was to be prevented and eliminated from the region. They unequivocally condemned all acts, methods and practices of terrorism as criminal and deplored their impact on life and property, social economic development, political stability, regional and international peace and co-operation. They recognized the importance of the principles laid down in UN Resolution 2625 which among others required that each State should refrain from organizing, instigating, assisting or participating in acts of civil strife or terrorist acts in another State or acquiesing in organized activities within its territory directed towards the commission of such acts.

12. The Heads of State or Government expressed their concern at the crisis facing the United Nations system. They reiterated their deep commitment to the purposes and principles of the United Nations Charter and their support for and faith in the United Nations as the most important international forum for addressing issues of peace, disarmament and development and an essential instrument for bringing about justice and equity in international political and economic relations. They resolved to concert their efforts in all multilateral fora within the United Nations system to preserve and strengthen

the Organisation and to prevent erosion of its role, functions and principles.

13. The Heads of State or Government reiterated their deep commitment to the principles and objectives of the Non-aligned Movement and underlined the historic role the Movement had been playing in strengthening international peace, promoting development, establishing equitable and just economic relations and strengthening international co-operation in all fields. The success of the Harare Summit of the Non-aligned countries was yet another demonstration of the strength and unity of the Movement and the increasing respect that it had come to command in the international community. They affirmed full support for the decisions adopted at the Summit and called for their early implementation.

14. The leaders of the South Asian countries were convinced that an environment of peace, security and respect for international law was essential for their growth and stability. Unfortunately, this environment had become increasingly adverse for the pursuit of their cherished goals. The international political scene was marred by strife and tension due to Great Power policies and practices of domination and intervention as well as the increased resort to the treat or use of force, aggression, occupation, pressure, economic coercion and interference in flagrant violation of the principles and purposes of the Charter of the United Nations. The arms race, particularly the nuclear arms race, had escalated to a point where it jeopardizes the most fundamental of all human rights - the right to live.

15. The Heads of State or Government noted with deep disappointment that the promise held out by the Reykjavik Summit could not be realized. They, however, noted with satisfaction that the proposals made at the Summit were still on the table. They expressed the earnest hope that the negotiations would be resumed without delay so that a decisive step could be taken towards realizing the ultimate goal of eliminating nuclear weapons altogether. The Heads of State or government called for the early conclusion of a Comprehensive Test Ban Treaty.

16. The Heads of State or Government were deeply concerned that the world economy continued to be in the throes of crisis, with particularly harsh and severe consequences for the economies and development prospects and aspirations of the developing countries. They endorsed the Declaration of the SAARC Ministerial Meeting on International Economic Issues held in Islamabad and its analysis of the exceptionally adverse external economic environment which retards the development of the South Asian and other developing countries. These negative factors include depressed commodity prices, rising protectionism, global recession, lower export earnings, net outflow of financial resources from developing countries and an aggravated debt crisis.

17. The Heads of State or Government noted that the rates of growth in the developed countries had turned out to be much lower than what was earlier projected and that the projection for future growth in these countries was not at all encouraging. They expressed their concern at the implications of these trends for the development prospects of the developing countries. They welcomed the recent

recognition by the developed countries that the chronic problems of massive payment imbalances, high interest rates, unstable exchange rates and high unemployment are structural in nature. In view of global interdependence, the co-ordination of macro-economic policies, contemplated at the Tokyo Summit of the seven major industrialized countries, cannot be effective in achieving sustained global economic growth unless it encompasses the developing countries.

18. The leaders urged that the recent retreat from multilateralism should be urgently reversed through a revival of the North-South dialogue which is responsive to the changed circumstances in the world economy. This must include a process of reform of monetary and financial system, through an International Conference on Money and Finance for Development, and urgent measures for preserving and strengthening the multilateral trading system. In the search for revival of global growth, priority must be accorded to exploiting the vast potential for expanded production, consumption and trade which exists in the developing countries. In all these endeavours, high priority should be accorded to supporting the development of the least developed countries, in particular, through the full and effective implementation of the Substantial New Programme of Action for the Least Developed Countries for the 1980s.

19. The Heads of State or Government noted with satisfaction that at the SAARC Ministerial Meeting on International Economic Issues a number of priority objectives of the SAARC countries have been identified. These include: enlarged concessional

assistance, the doubling in three years of the financial flows for the development of developing countries, amelioration of official debts, trade liberalization, especially in textiles and agriculture, commodity price stabilization, transfer of technology and special treatment for least developed SAARC countries. The Heads of State or Government agreed that the SAARC members should closely and regularly consult and co-operate in relevant international economic conferences and institutions in order to promote the above mentioned objectives. They recognised that an important opportunity in this context would be provided by UNCTAD VII.

20. The Heads of State or Government were of the view that the forthcoming New Round of Multilateral Trade Negotiations posed a challenge for their countries as well as an opportunity to accelerate their development through the expansion of their exports. They underlined the importance of the effective implementation with immediate effect and continuance until the formal completion of the negotiations, of the commitment to observe a standstill on protectionist measures and to roll these back under multilateral surveillance. They also expected that the principles of transparency and differential and more favourable treatment for the developing countries would be applied systematically and in concrete terms in the negotiations. They decided to concert their positions in these negotiations with a view to deriving maximum benefits from them in accordance with their national objectives and priorities.

21. The Heads of State or Government expressed their conviction that the Bangalore Summit had helped in

consolidating the gains of regional co-operation activities so far undertaken by SAARC while, at the same time, exploring new avenues and possibilities for such co-operation. The Bangalore Summit had made a significant contribution to strengthening and streamlining the institutional basis for such co-operation.

22. The Heads of State or Government reiterated their determination and will to expand and strengthen their co-operation under SAARC. They underlined their belief that SAARC reflected a resurgence of the South Asian consciousness which had inspired the peoples of this region over several millenia. The leaders expressed their deep conviction that South Asian regional co-operation would not only have a salutary effect on bilateral relations between the countries of the region, but also impart strength and stability to these relations.

23. The Heads of State or Government of Bangladesh, Bhutan, Maldives, Nepal, Pakistan and Sri Lanka were deeply appreciative of the exemplary manner in which the Prime Minister of India discharged his responsibilities as Chairman of the Meeting. They expressed their profound gratitude for the warm and gracious hospitality extended to them by the Government and people of India and for the excellent arrangements made for the Meeting.

Joint Press Release

Joint Press Release Issued an November 17, 1986 at the End of the Second SAARC Summit, Bangalore.

1. The President of Bangladesh, the King of Bhutan, the Prime Minister of India, the President of Maldives, the King of Nepal, the Prime Minister of Pakistan and the President of Sri Lanka met in Bangalore on 16 and 17 November, 1986.

2. They issued the Bangalore Declaration. A Memorandum of Understanding on the Establishment of the SAARC Secretariat was signed by the Foreign Ministers of the SAARC countries in their presence.

3. They welcomed the announcement by His Majesty's Government of Nepal that the Secretariat would be inaugurated in Kathmandu on 16 January, 1987. They decided that the first Secretary-General of the SAARC Secretariat, His Excellency Mr. Abul Ahsan, would assume charge of this office from that date.

4. They also considered several new ideas for expanding and strengthening the co-operative programmes under SAARC. While approving the following ideas in principle they directed that these be elaborated and concretized through expert level examination to be completed by March 1987, so that the reports there on could be considered at the next Meeting of the Council of Ministers :

   (a) A South Asian Broadcasting Programme covering both radio and television should be launched.

   (b) In keeping with the emphasis that the Heads of State or Government have laid on people-to-people contacts concrete steps should be taken to facilitate tourism in the region, including facilities for limited convertibility of national currencies for tourists from SAARC countries.

(c) The Heads of State or Government emphasized the importance they attach to students, scholars and researchers in their countries having ready access to reliable and up-to-date information on technical, scientific and developmental matters. This need could be best met by a SAARC Documentation Centre as the repository of such information.

(d) The Heads of State or Government considered that it was essential to promote increasing cross-fertilization of ideas through greater interaction among students, scholars and academics in the SAARC countries. They, therefore, directed that a concerted programme of exchange of scholars be formulated and action taken for an early institution of SAARC scholarships, SAARC Fellowships and SAARC Chairs.

(e) The Heads of State or Government stressed that the idealism of youth must be harnessed for regional co-operative programmes. Nothing would be more conducive to the resurgence of South Asian consciousness than the involvement of the youth of each country with the development programmes of the other. An Organized Volunteers Programme should be established in SAARC under which volunteers from one country would be able to work in other countries in the fields of agriculture and forestry extension work.

5. The Heads of State or Government recalled that the planners of the SAARC countries had met in 1983. This had provided a useful opportunity for an exchange of ideas and experience in the formulation of development strategies and methods of plan implementation. They directed that another meeting

of the planners of the SAARC member countries be convened at the earliest.

6. The Heads of State or Government took note of the recommendations of the Standing Committee on the financing of the institutional costs of regional institutions. They decided that for regional institutions where all the Member States are directly involved and benefit, the formula proposed by the Standing Committee should be used. However, in the case of projects which affect only a certain number of Member States, the formula should be used as an indicative one, which could be suitably modified on the basis of consultations among the Member States.

7. The Heads of State or Government also decided that the next Meeting of the Council of Ministers would be held in India in May 1987. They directed that this Meeting should undertake a detailed review of the proposals for the establishment of regional institutions. The member countries which have undertaken to prepare concept papers, pre-feasibility or feasibility studies on these proposals, should complete them well before the convening of the Meeting. The SAARC Secretariat should establish and submit to the Ministers, an order of priority among these proposals having regard to their costs, benefits, readiness for implementation, and other relevant factors.

8. The Heads of State or Government gratefully accepted the offer of the King of Nepal to host the Third SAARC Summit in 1987.

9. They also accepted with gratitude the offer of the President of Sri Lanka to host the Fourth SAARC Summit in Sri Lanka in 1988.

6

Declaration of the Third SAARC Summit, Kathmandu

The Kathmandu Declaration of the Heads of State or Government of the member countries of the South Asian Association for Regional Cooperation issued on November 4, 1987.

Introduction

1. The President of Bangladesh, the King of Bhutan, the Prime Minister of India, the President of Maldives, the King of Nepal, the Prime Minister of Pakistan and the President of Sri Lanka assembled for the Third Summit of the South Asian Association for Regional Cooperation (SAARC) in Kathmandu on 2-4 November, 1987.
2. The Heads of State or Government recalled with pleasure the launching of SAARC which marked the beginning of a new era of regional cooperation for the promotion of peace and progress, mutual trust

and goodwill in South Asia and underlined the importance of annual meetings at their level, as a prime mover, in consolidating and accelerating the pace and process of overall social, economic and cultural development in the region. They renewed their commitment to the SAARC Charter. They reiterated their desire of promoting peace, stability, amity and progress in the region through strict adherence to the principles of the United Nations Charter and Nonalignment, particularly respect for the principles of sovereign equality, territorial integrity, national independence, non-use of force and non-interference in the internal affairs of other States and peaceful settlement of disputes.

3. The Heads of State or Government emphasized that a fundamental goal of SAARC was to promote the welfare of the peoples of South Asia and to provide them with the opportunity to live in dignity and realise their full potential. They were conscious of the formidable tasks ahead of eradicating poverty, hunger, disease, illiteracy and unemployment and alleviation of environmental degradation facing South Asia today. They were convinced that the peoples and governments of South Asia could, acting in unison, surmount these challenges.

4. The Heads of State or Government expressed their faith in and commitment to the principles and purposes enshrined in the United Nation Charter. They further believed that the United Nations has an important role to play in promoting universal trust, understanding and concerted actions for the attainment of lasting peace, global development and general disarmament. They reiterated their concern at the crisis facing the United Nations. They expressed

their commitment to the multilateral negotiating process and called upon all states to help strengthen the UN system. They reaffirmed their belief that SAARC will reinforce this process by promoting South Asian cooperation.

5. The Heads of State or Government also reaffirmed their deep commitment to the principles and objectives of the Non-Aligned Movement. They underscored the validity of its philosophy and the historic role the Movement has been playing and continues to play in strengthening world peace and harmony as well as in promoting development with justice and equity. They also noted that institutionalization and strengthening of regional cooperation in South Asia had further nurtured the spirit of South-South cooperation on the basis of mutual respect, equity and common benefit. They expressed satisfaction over the result of the Ministerial Conference on Nonaligned Countries held in Pyongyang in June 1987 and urged the Non-aligned and other developing countries to take action to implement effectively the Pyongyang Declaration and Plan of Action on South-South Cooperation.

6. The Heads of State or Government recognised that the external environment had a critical bearing on the development of the economies of the South Asian Region. They noted with deep concern that growth in the world economy had again slowed down with adverse consequences for South Asia and other developing countries, especially for the least developed and landlocked countries. They observed that equitable participation of the developing countries in international trading and economic systems and in arrangements for the coordination of

global macro economic policies was essential for enhancing prospects and performance of the world economy.

7. The South Asian leaders noted that the world economy had long suffered from a structural disequilibrium. The pace of global economic expansion had further slowed down. The downward trend in commodity prices had continued. The net export earnings had fallen aggravating payment imbalances in developing countries. The terms of trade had further deteriorated with enormous losses to developing countries. At the same time, the diminishing financial flows to developing countries remained unchanged with contraction in new lendings and growing burden of debt servicing. In fact there had been a reverse flow of resources from developing to developed countries. The trade conflicts had also sharpened with the rise of protectionism thus further weakening the international trading system and eroding the principle of special and differential treatment in favour of developing countries.

8. The Heads of State or Government reiterated the urgent need for resumption of North-South Dialogue with a view to promoting coordinated actions by developed and developing countries to channel trade surpluses for development, revive growth in flagging economies, overcome debt difficulties, expand export access to the developing countries and stabilise commodity prices, regulate capital flows and exchange rates more closely, and provide emergency relief and assistance to the poorest countries. They called for an early convening of the International Conference on Money and Finance for Development.

They also stressed the need for preserving and liberalizing the multilateral trading system with renewed efforts both within and outside the GATT Uruguay Round of Multilateral Trade Negotiations. They also underscored the importance of the developed countries fully respecting the commitments made in Punta del Este on "standstill and rollback" and called for the early and effective implementation of this commitment. The Heads of State or Government also reviewed the outcome of UNCTAD VII. They hoped that UNCTAD would play an increasingly effective role in promoting harmonious and equitable international economic relations.

9. The Heads of State or Government reaffirmed the need for special measures in favour of the least developed countries in order to strengthen their resource capabilities and structural transformation and urged the international community, in the light of recent decisions at UNCTAD VII, to speed-up tangible assistance including increased resource flows to these countries within the framework of the Substantial New Program of Action (SNPA) for the Least Developed Countries for 1980s.

10. The Heads of State or Government expressed concern at the deteriorating international political environment which was due to great power policies and practices of domination and intervention as well as the increased resort to threat or use of force, aggression, occupation, pressure, economic coercion and interference in violation of the principles and purposes of the Charter of the United Nations. These destabilising measures were creating a climate

detrimental to the policies of peace, goodwill, stability, prosperity and respect for each other.

11. The Heads of State or Government believed that the escalation in military expenditure was a major constraint on world development. In this regard they noted that the UN Conference on Disarmament and Development had clearly established a link between disarmament and development and had provided a valuable frame work for future action in this vital area.

12. They welcomed the understanding reached between the United States and the Soviet Union on Intermediate Nuclear Forces. This should be a precursor of further accords between them to reduce drastically their strategic nuclear missiles and to refrain from extending the arms race to Outer Space. They called for the early conclusion in the Geneva Conference on Disarmament of a Comprehensive Test Ban Treaty and a Convention to Ban Chemical Weapons. They declared their intention to continue their efforts to contribute to the realisation of the objective of halting the nuclear arms race and eliminating nuclear weapons. They declared their resolve to support every effort to conclude a treaty prohibiting vertical and horizontal proliferation of nuclear weapons.

13. The Heads of State or Government expressed their deep concern at the fast and continuing degradation of the environment, including extensive destruction of forests, in the South Asian region. They also noted that South Asia was afflicted with such natural disasters as floods, droughts, landslides, cyclones, tidal waves which have had a particularly severe

impact recently, causing immense human suffering. At the same time they expressed concern over the danger posed by the global sea level rise and its effects on South Asian countries. These natural disasters and the degradation of the environment were severely undermining the development process and prospects of the member countries. They, therefore, decided to intensify regional cooperation with a view to strengthening their disaster management capabilities. They also decided to commission a study for the protection and preservation of the environment and to the causes and consequences of natural disasters in a well-planned comprehensive framework. They entrusted the Secretary-General with this task.

14. The Heads of State or Government reaffirmed their conviction that the region being most populous in the world and having age-old socio-cultural links, rich and varied human and natural resources, offered immense scope and potential for regional cooperation and that the growing interaction among its people had added stimulus towards this end. They reiterated their determination to pursue their individual and collective efforts for the optimal utilisation of the vast human and untapped natural and other material resources.

15. The Heads of State or Government reviewed with satisfaction the progress made so far in the implementation of the SAARC Integrated Programme of Action and emphasised the need to further consolidate and streamline the process. They were conscious of the need to exercise greater discretion in the selection of activities in different sectors. They took note of the criteria and procedures relating to

administrative structuring and financing of regional institutions endorsed by the SAARC Council of Ministers. They directed that the establishment of such regional institutions should proceed only after taking into account their viability and benefits to the member countries with due consideration to economy and efficiency.

16. The Heads of State or Government expressed satisfaction at the launching of the SAARC Audio Visual Exchange programme coinciding with the opening of the Third SAARC Summit in Kathmandu. While taking note of the dates for the institution of the SAARC Chairs, Fellowships and Scholarships and the commencement of Organised Tourism among SAARC member countries, they directed that the schemes for the SAARC Documentation Centre and the SAARC Youth Volunteer Programme be implemented at the earliest.

17. The Heads of State or Government noted with satisfaction the signing of the Agreement establishing a South Asian Food Security Reserve and expressed confidence that this will provide a much-needed cushion against food shortages and scarcity situations in the region.

18. The Heads of State or Government expressed happiness at the signing of the SAARC Regional Convention on Suppression of Terrorism and considered it a historic step towards the prevention and elimination of terrorism from the region. In this regard, they also reiterated their unequivocal condemnation of all acts, methods and practice of terrorism as criminal and expressed their abhorrence of their impact on life and property, socio-economic

development, political stability, regional peace and cooperation.

19. The Heads of State or Government reaffirmed their agreement to expand SAARC activities in other concrete areas of cooperation in order to ensure more tangible benefits from SAARC to the peoples of the region. They were convinced that regional cooperation could be consolidated and expanded on the basis of growing regional complementarities and inter dependence. They believed that the SAARC long-term perspective should, therefore, focus on measures to expand and strengthen such areas of regional complementarities and interdependence not only through formulation and implementation of more concrete and action-oriented programmes but also through coordination of national policies and approaches for finding common solutions to their common problems.

20. The Heads of State or Government welcomed the first annual review of the Situation of Children in the SAARC member countries. They reiterated their commitment made in the Bangalore Declaration to accord highest priority to the needs of children in national development planning and emphasised that more intensified action should be taken for the welfare and well-being of children. They further reiterated their call for an early conclusion and adoption of a United Nations Convention on the Rights of the Child.

21. The Heads of State or Government expressed their satisfaction at the establishment of the SAARC Secretariat in Kathmandu, strengthening further the process of regional cooperation in South Asia. They

expressed their gratitude to His Majesty King Birendra Bir Bikram Shah Dev for most graciously inaugurating the SAARC Secretariat.

22. The Heads of State or Government were conscious of the aspirations of the peoples of South Asia to communicate and cooperate with each other at the people-to-people level. They recognised that academics, researchers, non-governmental organizations and others have an important role to play in promoting the SAARC spirit and giving impetus to regional programmes and projects. They further observed that the interest and enthusiasm so far demonstrated by the increased interactions and exchange of information at the inter-governmental level should be capitalised and translated into tangible programmes and projects. They recognised the vast potential for the generation of friendship, goodwill and trust through interactions between the peoples which would foster harmonious relations in South Asia.

23. The Heads of State or Government expressed their deep conviction that the Kathmandu Summit has further consolidated the gains of SAARC and given a renewed thrust and direction to the future course of regional cooperation. They were also convinced that the Kathmandu Summit has helped to create an atmosphere conducive to strengthening this process, besides generating further goodwill and friendship among the member countries in the larger interest of the region.

24. The Heads of State or Government were conscious that SAARC should be increasingly oriented to the people's needs and aspirations so that the masses of

the region could be drawn to a greater extent into the mainstream of SAARC activities. This, they firmly held, would help bring about a qualitative improvement in the general atmosphere of the region contributing to peace, friendship and cooperation in the areas.

25. The Heads of State or Government reiterated their firm commitment to the spirit and objectives with which the South Asian Association for Regional Cooperation was launched and reaffirmed their determination to work, individually and collectively, towards the attainment of these objectives.

26. The Heads of State or Government of Bangladesh, Bhutan, India, Maldives, Pakistan and Sri Lanka were deeply appreciative of the exemplary manner in which His Majesty the King of Nepal discharged his responsibilities as Chairman of the Meeting. They expressed their profound gratitude for the warm and gracious hospitality extended to them by His Majesty's Government and the people of Nepal and for the excellent arrangements made for the Meeting.

****

Joint Press Release

Joint Press Release Issued on November 4, 1987 at the End of the Third SAARC Summit, Kathmandu.

1. The President of Bangladesh, the King of Bhutan, the Prime Minister of India, the President of Maldives, the King of Nepal, the Prime Minister of Pakistan and President of Sri Lanka met in Kathmandu during November 2-4, 1987. Their meeting was marked by warmth, cordiality and mutual understanding.

2. They issued the Kathmandu Declaration providing a renewed thrust and direction to the future course of regional cooperation in South Asia.

3. They considered several issues of common concern, both regional and international, ad assessed the overall progress in the context of SAARC objectives.

4. They expressed their happiness at the signing of the SAARC Regional Convention on Suppression of Terrorism and the Agreement establishing South Asian Food Reserve by the Foreign Ministers of the SAARC Member States in their presence. they firmly believed that the Convention and the Agreement constituted landmarks in their collective endeavours to eradicate terrorism and hunger from the region.

5. They declared their intention to initiate the process of dealing with the causes and consequences of natural disasters and decided to commission a study on natural disasters and the protection and preservation of the environment in a well planned and comprehensive framework. They entrusted the Secretary-General with this task.

6. They expressed their satisfaction with the progress achieved in the implementation of the Integrated Programme of Action in the eleven agreed areas of cooperation and also with the concrete programmes related to the Five New Ideas identified at the last Summit for expanding and strengthening cooperative programmes under SAARC.

7. They also reaffirmed their view that measures for expanding regional cooperation should be progressively carried out within a broad framework of long-term perspective and stressed, in particular,

the need for further consolidation and rationalization of the on-going activities pursued within SAARC framework.

8. The Heads of State or Government emphasized the need for strengthening inter-governmental efforts with increased people-to-people cooperation and called for greater participation of the Non-Governmental Organizations (NGOs), including professional bodies in the private sector, in the process of promoting socio-economic and cultural development of South Asia as envisaged in the SAARC Charter, under the auspices of the SAARC Secretariat.

9. They further welcomed the establishment of the SAARC Secretariat in Kathmandu as well as the assumption of office by the SAARC Secretary-General with effect from 16 January, 1987 and considered these as important events in strengthening the institutional framework of regional cooperation in South Asia. They expressed their appreciation to His Majesty's Government of Nepal at the cooperation and assistance extended and facilities provided to the SAARC Secretariat.

10. The Heads of State or Government took note of the Report submitted by the Council of Ministers relating, inter alia, to administrative structuring and financing of regional institutions and directed that for economy and efficiency all sectoral programmes should justify the establishment of such regional institutions.

11. They instructed that in its examination of the question of the admission of new members and the grant of observer/guest status in the Association, the

Standing Committee should also include the aspect of the establishment of relations with similar organisations.

12. They gratefully accepted the offer of the President of Sri Lanka to host the Fourth SAARC Summit in 1988 in Sri Lanka.

13. They also gratefully accepted the offer of the Prime Minister of the Islamic Republic of Pakistan to host the Fifth SAARC Summit in Pakistan in 1989.

14. The Heads of State or Government of Bangladesh, Bhutan, India, Maldives, Pakistan and Sri Lanka were deeply appreciative of the exemplary manner in which His Majesty the King of Nepal discharged his responsibilities as Chairman of the Meeting. They expressed their profound gratitude for the warm and gracious hospitality extended to them by His Majesty's Government and the people of Nepal and for the excellent arrangements made for the Meeting.

7

Declaration of the Fourth SAARC Summit, Islamabad

The Islamabad Declaration of the Heads of State or Government of the Member Countries of South Asian Association for Regional Cooperation issued on 31st December 1988.

Introduction

1. The President of Bangladesh, the King of Bhutan, the Prime Minister of India, the President of Maldives, the King of Nepal, the Prime Minister of Pakistan and the President of Sri Lanka met at the Fourth Summit of the South Asian Association for Regional Cooperation at Islamabad from 29-31 December, 1988.
2. The Heads of State of Government expressed their deep satisfaction at the progress achieved by the Association since the last Summit. They reiterated their commitment to the SAARC Charter and renewed their determination to cooperate in

promoting the welfare of the peoplesof South Asia and to improving their quality of life by eradicating poverty, hunger, disease, illiteracy, unemployment and environmental degradation.

3. They recalled that their countries were linked by cultural, social and historical ties and they had at their disposal substantial human and natural resources. They recognised that these provided a sound basis as well as immense opportunities for regional cooperation. They therefore expressed their determination to make optimal use of their resources for the benefit of their people by working jointly to pursue their shared objectives. They were aware that by acting in concert they could realise the full potential for regional progress, taking into account complementarities and growing inter-dependence.

4. The leaders endorsed the decision of the Council of Ministers that any country in the region subscribing to the objectives and principles of the SAARC Charter may be admitted as a member of the Association by a unanimous decision of the Heads of State of Government.

5. The Heads of State of Government expressed satisfaction at the progress so far made in the implementation of the SAARC Integrated Programme of Action. They underlined the need for closer cooperation in the activities undertaken under this programme. They took note of the measures to streamline and re-orient various SAARC activities to make them more action-oriented so as to improve the quality of life of their peoples. They directed that the Secretary General may submit recommendation to the Standing Committee which should in turn decide

how to streamline SAARC activities and make them more effective. They welcomed the establishment of the SAARC Agricultural Information Centre (SAIC), as well as the steps being taken for the establishment of other regional institutions.

6. The Heads of State of Government lauded the smooth functioning of the SAARC Audio Visual Exchange (SAVE) Programme which had proved to be a useful medium for promoting a South Asian consciousness amongst the peoples of the region. They decided that SAVE Programmes should also emphasise social, economic and technical themes. They also noted with satisfaction the successful launching of the Youth Volunteers Programme and the SAARC Chairs, Fellowships and Scholarships Scheme. They decided that Education may be included as an agreed area of cooperation.

7. The Heads of State of Government expressed satisfaction that the South Asian Food Security Reserve had become operational on 12 August 1988. The Reserve would serve as a cushion against food shortages and was a tangible manifestation of the spirit of cooperation in the region.

8. The Heads of State of Government noted with satisfaction that the SAARC Convention on Suppression of Terrorism had been ratified and had come into effect on 22 August 1988, thus reflecting the sincere desire on the part of the Member States to enter into meaningful cooperation to eliminate the scourge of terrorism from the South Asian region. They called for the adoption of enabling measures by Member States to implement the Convention at the earliest.

9. The Heads of State of Government expressed grave concern over the growing magnitude and the serious effects of drug abuse, particularly among young people, and drug trafficking. They recognised the need for urgent and effective measures to eradicate this evil ad decided to declare the year 1989 as the "SAARC Year for Combating Drug Abuse and Drug Trafficking". They agreed to launch a concerted campaign, as suited to the situation in their respective countries, to significantly augment SAARC efforts to eliminate drug abuse and drug trafficking. These included closer cooperation in creating a greater awareness of the hazards of drug abuse, exchange of expertise, sharing of intelligence information, stringent measures to stop trafficking in drugs and introduction of more effective laws. They directed that the Technical Committee concerned should examine the possibility of a Regional Convention on Drug Control.

10. The Heads of State or Government expressed their deep sense of sorrow and profound sympathy at the loss of valuable lives and extensive damage to property suffered during the year by Bangladesh, India, Nepal and Pakistan as a result of unprecedented floods, cyclones and earthquakes. In this connection, they recalled their earlier decision at Kathmandu in November, 1987 to intensify regional cooperation with a view to strengthening their disaster management capabilities and took note of the recommendations of the meeting of the SAARC Group of Experts on the Study on the Causes and Consequences of Natural Disasters and the Protection and Preservation of the Environment, that met in Kathmandu in July 1988. They expressed the

conviction that identification of measures and programmes as envisaged by the Group of Experts would supplement national, bilateral, regional and global efforts to deal with the increasingly serious problems being faced by the region as a result of the recurrence of natural disasters and the continuing degradation of the environment. They urged that the study should be completed in the shortest period of time so that it could provide a basis for the member countries to draw up an action plan for meaningful cooperation amongst the Member States. They decided that a joint study be undertaken on the "Greenhouse Effect" and its impact on the region.

11. The Heads of State or Government noted with satisfaction that modalities for studies to be carried out for cooperation in the areas of trade, manufactures and services had been worked out by a Group of Experts, which met in Islamabad recently. They emphasised the need for the completion of the studies within the agreed time schedule. They directed that the Fourth Meeting of Planners should examine the possibility of cooperation in agreed areas of trade, manufactures and services, which would promote the objectives of meeting the basic needs of the peoples of the region. The report of the Planners should be considered at the next Council of Ministers meeting, with a view to making specific recommendations to the next Summit.

12. The Heads of State or Government reviewed the progress on the Situation of Children in SAARC countries. They reiterated their commitment made in the Bangalore Declaration to accord the highest priority to the needs of children in national development planning and stressed that the concept

of Human Resource Development should lay particular emphasis on the welfare and well-being of children, especially in the literacy and health spheres. They called for the conclusion and adoption of the UN Convention on the Rights of the Child in 1989. They decided to declare 1990 as the "SAARC Year of the Girl Child".

13. The Heads of State or Government noted with satisfaction the effective functioning of the SAARC Secretariat and its role in coordinating SAARC activities. They also noted that a Headquarters Agreement had been signed between the Secretariat and the host Government. They thanked His Majesty's Government of Nepal for the assistance and cooperation extended to the Secretariat.

14. The Heads of State or Government noted that the decision to involve regional NGOs or professional bodies in SAARC activities, taken at the Fifth Session of the Council of Ministers, pursuant to the direction given by the Kathmandu Declaration, was an important step towards the promotion of people-to-people contact which has always been emphasised by the Association.

15. The Heads of State or Government stressed the need for closer and more frequent contacts among the peoples of SAARC. As a beginning, they decided that Supreme Court Judges and Members of the National Parliaments of each member State would be entitled to a special SAARC travel document which would exempt them from visas. They further directed the Council of Ministers to examine what other categories of persons should be given this facility and to submit their recommendations.

16. They further noted with satisfaction the mandate given to the Secretary General by the Council of Ministers at its Fifth Session on the question of contacting organisations with similar aims and purposes.

17. The Heads of State or Government expressed their determination to give concrete shape to the objectives of SAARC. In this context they emphasised the need to progressively carry out SAARC activities within a broad framework of a long-term perspective and to harmonize their efforts to ensure tangible benefits to the peoples of South Asia as a whole. They were conscious of the fact that all South Asian countries faced problems in varying degrees in areas such as food, clothing, shelter, education, primary health care, population planning and environmental protection. Towards this end they were of the view that all Member States should identity areas of core interest in their national perspective plans or prepare such plans and consolidate them into a regional plan to be called "SAARC-2000 : A Basic Needs Perspective", with specific targets to be met by the end of the century.

18. They recognised that Human Resource Development is one of the means of realizing these objectives. In this context they welcomed the offer of the Government of Pakistan to host a Centre for Human Resource Development and directed the Secretary-General to set up a Group of Experts from Member States to examine the proposal on the basis of a paper to be prepared by the Government of Pakistan and to submit its recommendations to the Standing Committee.

19. The Heads of State or Government reaffirmed their abiding commitment to the purposes and principles enshrined in the UN Charter, particularly those enjoining respect for the sovereign equality, territorial integrity and national independence, non-use or threat of use of force, non-interference in the internal affairs of other states and peaceful settlement of all disputes. They reiterated their faith in the United Nations as the most important forum for the maintenance of international peace and security and for the promotion of international cooperation aimed at the progress and prosperity of mankind.

20. The Heads of State or Government noted with satisfaction the relaxation of global tensions through intensified super-power dialogue on a broad range of international issues and welcomed the progress towards the resolution of protracted regional disputes and conflicts. They agreed that these developments had enhanced the prospects for disarmament, security, peace and progress for all peoples of the world. They appreciated the important role played by the United Nations in bringing about these positive changes in the international political environment. They also called upon all States to strengthen the capacity of the UN system in all respects to achieve the purpose of the UN Charter.

21. The Heads of State or Government reiterated their deep commitment to the principles and objectives of the Non-aligned Movement as an important force for strengthening world peace and harmony as well as for promoting development with justice and equity. In this context they expressed satisfaction over the results of the Ministerial Conference of the Non-aligned Movement held in Cyprus in September 1988

and expressed the hope the decisions of the Conference would contribute to the reduction of tensions and to the promotion of development. They hoped that the current discussions on the improvement in the methodology of the Non-Aligned Movement would result in strengthening the movement and enable it to play its role with greater effectiveness.

22. The Heads of State or Government believed that the escalation in military expenditure was a major constraint on world development. In this regard they noted that the UN Conference on Disarmament and Development had clearly established a link between disarmament and development and had provided a valuable framework for future action in this vital area. They urged that resources saved through disarmament measures should be diverted in particular to developing countries for development.

23. They welcomed the agreement between the United States and the Soviet Union on Intermediate Nuclear Force. They hoped this would be a precursor to further accords to reduce strategic nuclear arsenals drastically and to prevent an arms race in Outer Space. They called for the early conclusion in the Geneva Conference on Disarmament of a Comprehensive Test Ban Treaty and a Convention to Ban Chemical Weapons. They declared their intention to continue their efforts to contribute to the realization of the objective of halting the nuclear arms race and eliminating nuclear weapons. They declared their resolve to support every effort to conclude a treaty prohibiting vertical and horizontal proliferation of nuclear weapons.

24. The Heads of State or Government noted with deep concern the continued structural disequilibrium from which the world economy had long suffered. This had resulted in slower growth in the developing countries, downward trends in commodity prices, decline in the net export earnings of the developing countries and deterioration in their terms of trade. These developments combined with the overwhelming debt burdens, the reverse financial flows from the developing to the developed countries and the sharp rise of protectionism in the developed world had further aggravated the economic difficulties of the developing countries.

25. The Heads of State or Government emphasised the interdependent character of the economies of the developed and the developing countries. They called for the resumption of the North-South dialogue with a view to restructuring the international economic system and to establishing the New International Economic Order based on justice and equity. They called for coordinated actions by the developed and the developing counties to increase the net flow of developmental assistance, overcome debt difficulties, expand the access of the developing countries to the markets in developed countries, arrest the deterioration in terms of trade of the developing countries and stabilize commodity prices.

26. The Heads of State or Government reiterated the need for preserving and liberalizing the multilateral trading system with renewed efforts both within and outside the Uruguay Round of Multilateral Trade Negotiations. They also underscored the importance of the developed countries fully respecting and implementing the commitments made in Punta del

Este on "standstill and rollback" arrangements. They expressed concern that on account of differences between major trading entities on the question of agricultural subsidies, the Montreal Meeting on the midterm review of the Uruguay round was inconclusive. They particularly regretted that there was no progress in the negotiations on issues of major interest to developing countries such as trade in textiles and a Safeguard System. They were disappointed that on some of the issues of interest to developing countries on which there was agreement, particularly tropical products, it would not be possible even to implement the decisions taken, from the beginning of 1989 as envisaged. They emphasised that the development dimension must be taken into account in the negotiations on new issues, particularly services and intellectual property rights. They agreed to take concerted action to this end in the forthcoming negotiations.

27. The Heads of State or Government fully supported the call for the initiation of a comprehensive process for the preparation of an International Development Strategy for the Fourth United Nations Development Decade as well as the proposal of the Group of 77 for convening a Special Session of the General Assembly in 1990 to revive growth and development in the developing countries.

28. The Heads of State or Government reemphasized the need for increased resource flows and special measures in favour of the least developed countries within the Framework of the Substantial New Programme of Action (SNPA) for these countries. They supported the convening of a high level United Nations Conference on the least developed countries

in 1990 to review progress and formulate national and international policies and measures for accelerating the development process in the least developed countries during the 1990s, especially in order to help them achieve their long term socio-economic objectives.

29. The Heads of State or Government of Bangladesh, Bhutan, India, Maldives, Nepal and Sri Lanka expressed their deep appreciation for the exemplary manner in which Prime Minister of Pakistan chaired the meeting. They expressed their profound gratitude for the excellent arrangements made for the meeting and for the warm and generous hospitality extended to them by the Government and the people of Pakistan.

Joint Press Release

Joint Press Release Issued on December 31, 1988 at the End of Fourth SAARC Summit, Islamabad.

1. The President of Bangladesh, the King of Bhutan, the Prime Minister of India, the President of Maldives, the King of Nepal, the Prime Minister of Pakistan and the President of Sri Lanka met at the Fourth Summit of the South Asian Association for Regional Cooperation at Islamabad from 29-31 December, 1988. The meeting was marked by an atmosphere of mutual understanding and spirit of accommodation.

2. The Heads of State or Government reaffirmed their commitment to the principles and objectives of the Association enshrined in the SAARC Charter and renewed their determination to work collectively

towards the attainment of these objectives. They issued the Islamabad Declaration.

3. The Heads of State or Government were deeply shocked at the armed attack on the Republic of Maldives on 3rd November, 1988 aimed at destabilising the Government and taking over the country. They strongly condemned these acts of violence which disrupted the peace and security of a Member State. They expressed full solidarity with the Government of Maldives.

4. The Heads of State or Government expressed concern at the high incidence of drug production, trafficking and abuse. They decided to declare 1989 as the "SAARC Year Against Drug Abuse" in order to focus attention on drug-related problems facing the region. They called upon Members States to prepare and implement national programmes in this regard.

5. They welcomed the launching of SAARC Chairs, Fellowships and Scholarships schemes and the Youth Volunteers programme. They recognised that Education was one of the principal areas requiring urgent attention in the region and decided to include Education among the agreed areas of cooperation. For this purpose they decided to set up a Technical Committee and accepted the offer of Bangladesh to chair the Committee.

6. The Heads of State or Government agreed to launch "SAARC-2000-A Basic Needs Perspective" which calls for a perspective regional plan with specific targets to be met by the end of the century in areas of core interest such as food, clothing, shelter, education, primary health care, population planning

and environmental protection. In this context they welcomed the offer of the Government of Pakistan to host a Centre for Human Resource Development and directed the Secretary-General to convene an Expert Group Meeting of member countries to work out modalities for the realization of "SAARC 2000 - A Basic Needs Perspective".

7. The Heads of State or Government welcomed the idea of holding South Asian Festivals from time to time and accepted the offer of India to host the first such festival.

8. The Heads of State or Government directed the Standing Committee to examine the desirability of establishing a regional body to promote cultural links among Member States.

9. They welcomed the coming into force of the SAARC Regional Convention on Suppression of Terrorism. They stressed the importance of the adoption of enabling measures at the national level that would be necessary in order to fully implement the provisions of the Convention.

10. They welcomed the Agreement regarding the establishment of a South Asian Food Security Reserve in August this year which marked a major breakthrough in the common endeavours of the Governments of member countries of SAARC to assist each other in food emergency situations.

11. The Heads of State or Government expressed their satisfaction at the progress achieved in the implementation of the Integrated Programme of Action (IPA). They recognised the need for focusing attention on more concrete and result-oriented activities within the SAARC framework.

12. They welcomed the establishment of the SAARC Agriculture Information Centre (SAIC) at Dhaka and were of the view that proposals for the setting up of regional institutions, focusing on problems of common concern in the region, should be given priority.

13. They reiterated their earlier commitment to accord priority to the needs of children in national development plans. They decided to declare 1990 as the "SAARC Year of the Girl Child" and directed that specific programmes and activities be undertaken to increase public awareness of the problems of the girl child.

14. They expressed satisfaction at the progress in the studies underway regarding the feasibility of cooperation in areas of trade, manufactures and services. In the meanwhile they directed the Secretary-General to convene a special meeting of the Group of Coordinators to identify any specific areas where cooperation may be feasible immediately. They directed that the report of the Group should be presented to the next sessions of the Standing Committee and the Council of Ministers.

15. The Heads of State or Government expressed profound sorrow at the natural disasters suffered by Bangladesh, Nepal, India and Pakistan in 1988 and urged that the study on the Causes and Consequences of Natural Disasters and the Protection and Preservation of the Environment be completed in the shortest period of time so as to provide a rational basis for identifying areas keeping in view the potentials and possibilities of evolving a regional plan of action, particularly to strengthen disaster management capabilities and to protect and preserve the environment.

16. They expressed satisfaction at the concrete steps being taken for the implementation of the SAARC Audio Visual Exchange (SAVE) Programme. They directed that social, economic and technical themes should be given emphasis by the SAVE Programme.

17. Recalling the usefulness of the earlier Ministerial meeting on Women in Development held in India in 1986, the Heads of State or Government called for the holding of a second Ministerial level meeting and welcomed the offer of the Government of Pakistan to host the meeting.

18. They expressed satisfaction that pursuant to the direction given by the Kathmandu Declaration for enhancing people-to -people contact, concrete steps had been taken by including regional NGOs and professional bodies in SAARC activities.

19. They decided that any country in the region subscribing to the objectives and principles of the Charter may be admitted as a member of the Association by a unanimous decision of the Heads of State or Government.

20. The Heads of State or Government noted with satisfaction the effective functioning of the SAARC Secretariat and its role in coordinating SAARC activities. They appreciated the work of the SAARC Secretary-General in the discharge of his responsibilities and thanked His Majesty's Government of Nepal for the assistance and cooperation extended to the Secretariat.

21. The Heads of State or Government gratefully accepted the offer of the Government of Sri Lanka to host the Fifth SAARC Summit in Colombo in 1989.

22. The Heads of State or Government expressed their deep appreciation for the outstanding manner in which the Prime Minister of Pakistan had conducted the meetings as the Chairperson of the Fourth SAARC Summit. They also expressed profound gratitude for the gracious hospitality extended to them by the Government and people of the Islamic Republic of Pakistan and for the excellent arrangements made for the Conference.

8

Declaration of the Fifth SAARC Summit, Male'

The Male Declaration of the Heads of State or Government of the Member Countries ofAsian Association for Regional Cooperation issued on 23rd November, 1990.

1. The President of the People's Republic of Bangladesh, His Excellency Mr. Hussain Muhammad Ershad, the King of Bhutan, His Majesty King Jigme Singye Wangchuck, the Prime Minister of the Republic of India, His Excellency Mr. Chandra Shekhar, the President of the Republic of Maldives, His Excellency Mr. Maumoon Abdul Gayoom, the Prime Minister of Nepal, The Right Honourable Krishna Prasad Bhattarai, the Prime Minister of the Islamic Republic of Pakistan, His Excellency Mr. Mohammad Nawaz Sharif and the Prime Minister of the Democratic Socialist Republic of Sri Lanka, His Excellency Mr. Dingiri Banda Wijetunga met at the Fifth Summit of the South Asian Association for Regional Cooperation at Male' on 2123 November, 1990.

2. The Heads of State or Government reiterated that cooperation among the countries of South Asia was

necessary for improving the quality of life of the peoples of the region. They recalled their conviction that the objectives of peace and stability in South Asia could be best served by fostering mutual understanding, cooperation and good neighbourly relations. They reaffirmed their commitment to the purposes and principles of the South Asian Association for Regional Cooperation and renewed their resolve to intensify cooperation under its aegis in pursuit of their common objectives.

3. The Heads of State or Government stressed their desire to promote peace, stability, amity and progress in the region through strict adherence to the principles of the United Nations Charter and the Nonaligned Movement, particularly respect for the principles of sovereign equality, territorial integrity, national independence, nonuse of force, noninterference in the internal affairs of other States and peaceful settlement of disputes.

4. The Heads of State or Government expressed satisfaction that the launching of SAARC in 1985 and the initiatives under the Integrated Programme of Action for strengthening regional cooperation in South Asia had generated much enthusiasm and hope in their peoples, and that the South Asian consciousness necessary for the success of regional cooperation was gradually permeating the region. They reiterated their resolve to make optimal use of the positive forces of goodwill, trust and understanding existing among their peoples and to turn SAARC into a dynamic instrument for achieving its objectives and creating an order based on mutual respect, equity, cooperation and shared benefits.

5. The Heads of State or Government reviewed the status of children in South Asia and noted that the recent World Summit for Children had imparted a new impetus to the ongoing efforts in this field. They believed that relevant recommendations of the World Summit could be usefully incorporated into a Plan of Action in the South Asian context and its implementation should be reviewed annually. The guidelines for such Plan of Action could be prepared by a panel of experts to be appointed by the SecretaryGeneral and examined by the Technical Committee on Health and Population Activities. They also welcomed the adoption of the Convention on the Rights of the Child and its entry into force. They expressed the hope that those Member States, who have not already become party to the Convention, would do so at an early date.

6. The Heads of State or Government endorsed the recommendations made by the Second SAARC Ministerial Meeting on Women in Development held in Islamabad in June 1990. They noted with satisfaction the enthusiastic response in all Member States to their collective call for the observance of 1990 as the "SAARC Year of the Girl Child". They decided that in order to maintain focus on the problems of the Girl Child, the years 19912000 AD should be observed as the "SAARC Decade of the Girl Child".

7. The Heads of State or Government noted with satisfaction the growing regional cooperation in combating the problems of drug trafficking and drug abuse. They expressed serious concern over the growing linkages between drug trafficking and international arms trade and terrorist activities. They

agreed that observance of 1989 as the "SAARC Year for Combating Drug Abuse and Drug Trafficking" had had a profound impact in drawing attention to the menace and to the need for its elimination. They expressed satisfaction that following the decision of the Fourth SAARC Summit, the SAARC Convention on Narcotic Drugs and Psychotropic Substances had been signed at Male'. They urged the Member States to take early measures to ratify the convention for its entry into force. They were convinced that the Convention would help in making SAARC efforts in this area more effective.

8. They endorsed the decision of the Council of Ministers in regard to the timeframe for completion of the Regional Study on the Causes and Consequences of Natural Disasters and the Protection and Preservation of the Environment. They noted with satisfaction that the methodology for undertaking the Study on the 'Greenhouse Effect' and its impact on the region was likely to be finalized in the near future and desired that the Study itself be completed for consideration at the Sixth Summit. In this context, they noted that the destruction of rainforests, the world over, was contributing significantly to adverse climatic changes and this aspect should also be covered in the proposed Study. They expressed the hope that these Studies would lead to an action plan for meaningful cooperation in the field of Environment and Disaster Management.

9. Recognizing that environment had emerged as a major global concern, the Heads of State or Government noted with alarm the unprecedented climatic changes predicted by the Intergovernmental

Panel on Climate Change (IPCC). They urged the international community to mobilize additional finances and to make available appropriate technologies to enable the developing countries to face the new challenges arising from climate changes and sealevel rise. They agreed that Member Countries should coordinate their positions at international fora on this issue. They also decided to observe 1992 as the "SAARC Year of Environment".

10. The Heads of State or Government noted with satisfaction that the national studies on Trade, Manufactures and Services had been completed. They underlined the need for expeditious action for completing the Regional Study within the timeframe stipulated by the Council of Ministers. They expressed the hope that it would open new avenues of cooperation for the prosperity of the peoples of the region.

11. The Heads of State or Government approved the recommendations of the Council of Ministers regarding Special SAARC Travel Document and decided to launch the scheme.

12. The Heads of State or Government expressed concern that Member States were compelled to divert their scarce resources in combating terrorism. They called for expeditious enactment of enabling measures for the implementation of the SAARC Regional Convention on Suppression of Terrorism. They also urged Member States to continue to cooperate in accordance with the Convention.

13. The Heads of State or Government noted that as their countries stood on the threshold of the next millennium, the world was undergoing profound

transformations characterised by popular upsurge for democracy, liberty and exercise of human rights, lowering of ideological barriers and the relaxation of global tensions and progress towards disarmament and the resolution of a number of regional and global conflicts. There was also a welcome trend towards the opening up of the global economy and integration of national economies into the mainstream of the world economy. They further noted the trend of increasing integration of the pattern of global production, consumption and trade, growing multipolarity of the world economic structure and integration of the markets of the developed countries in order to maintain their technological lead and competitive edge. These changes presented new challenges and opened up new opportunities to the South Asian countries, as to the rest of the developing world. The Heads of State or Government were convinced that their mutual cooperation can be a critical factor in enabling them to pursue these objectives more effectively.

14. The Heads of State or Government, noting the vital importance of biotechnology for the longterm food security of developing countries as well as for medicinal purposes, decided that cooperation should be extended to this field and, in particular, to the exchange of expertise in genetic conservation and maintenance of germplasm banks. In this connection, they welcomed India's offer of training facilities and agreed that cooperation in the cataloguing of genetic resources stored in different SAARC countries would be mutually beneficial. Taking note of the proposal made by the Group of Fifteen Developing Countries (G15) for the establishment of a gene bank for

developing countries, they agreed to participate in this venture.

15. The Heads of State or Government welcomed the idea of setting up of a Fund for regional projects which could make available credit on easy terms for the identification and development of regional projects. They agreed that representatives of the national development banks of the Member Countries should get together to work out the precise modalities for the source of funds and the manner in which these could be related to joint venture projects. They accepted India's offer to host this meeting.

16. The Heads of State or Government regarded the recent developments in the Gulf as the most unfortunate aberration from the present trend of detente, cooperation and peaceful settlement of disputes. They reaffirmed their adherence to UN Security Council Resolutions on this issue. While emphasizing the need for a peaceful solution of the issue, they called for immediate and unconditional withdrawal of Iraqi forces from Kuwait and the restoration of its legitimate Government. They stated that the Gulf crisis had dealt a severe blow to their economies. They needed massive international assistance to compensate the loss suffered by them due to a sharp decline in remittances, setback to their exports and severe strain on their balance of payments position imposed by increased oil prices. They recognized the potentiality of cooperation among themselves for mitigating the impact of these adverse consequences.

17. The Heads of State or Government noted with satisfaction that the initiative of the Government of

the Maldives for the Protection and Security of Small States at the UN in 1989, which they all supported, had also received overwhelming support of the international community. They agreed that, because of their particular problems, small states merited special measures of support in safeguarding their independence and territorial integrity.

18. The Heads of State or Government expressed the hope that the talks between the two Super Powers on arms control would culminate in the conclusion of an agreement for substantial reduction in their nuclear arsenals leading to the total elimination of nuclear weapons. While welcoming the measures being considered for arms reduction at the global level, they were convinced that the objective could be best achieved through the promotion of mutual trust and confidence among the Member States. They underlined the inherent relationship between disarmament and development and called upon all countries, especially those possessing the largest nuclear and conventional arsenals, to rechannel additional financial resources, human energy and creativity into development. They expressed their support for the banning of chemical weapons and early conclusion of a Comprehensive Test Ban Treaty. In this context, they welcomed the convening of the UN Conference in January 1991 to consider amendments to the Partial Test Ban Treaty to convert it into a Comprehensive Nuclear Test Ban Treaty.

19. The Heads of State or Government expressed concern that the international economic environment for the developing countries had been characterised by negative resource flows, high trade barriers, serious external debt problems and high interest rates. The

need of SAARC countries for increased concessional resources and technology as well as access to markets for their exports could not, therefore, be under estimated. They called for collective efforts based on mutuality of interest and felt that regular NorthSouth consultations were essential for ensuring equitable management of global interdependence.

20. The Heads of State or Government recalled the usefulness of the First Ministerial Meeting on International Economic Issues held in Islamabad in 1986. They agreed that the second such Ministerial Meeting be held in India in 1991 to review the outcome of the Uruguay Round and to coordinate positions at international conferences including the U.N. Conference on Environment and Development, 1992.

21. Notwithstanding the continuing efforts on the international economic plane, the Heads of State or Government emphasised the pressing need for the Ministerial Meeting to address itself vigorously to the objective of selfreliance. They directed the Ministers to prepare a strategy for mobilising regional resources which would encourage and strengthen individual and collective self reliance in the region.

22. The Heads of State or Government expressed their support for the Paris Declaration (1990) and the Programme of Action adopted by the Second United Nations Conference on the Least Developed Countries. They called upon the international community to contribute to the successful implementation of the Programme of Action which is of special importance for the socioeconomic development of the region.

23. The Heads of State or Government recognized the imperative need for providing a better habitat to the peoples of South Asia through optimum utilization of indigenous technology, knowhow and material, and decided that 1991 be observed as the "SAARC Year of Shelter".

24. The Heads of State or Government noted that millions of disabled persons lived in the SAARC region and immediate action was required to reduce their sufferings and to improve their quality of life. They decided to observe 1993 as the "SAARC Year of Disabled Persons".

25. The Heads of State or Government were particularly happy that the Fifth SAARC Summit coincided with the Twenty Fifth Anniversary of the Independence of the Maldives which provided them with the opportunity to express their solidarity with the people and the Government of the Maldives. They expressed their conviction that the Male' Summit had helped in consolidating the gains of regional cooperation and in strengthening the institutional base of SAARC.

26. The Heads of State or Government gratefully accepted the offer of the Government of Sri Lanka to host the Sixth SAARC Summit in 1991.

27. The Heads of State or Government of Bangladesh, Bhutan, India, Nepal, Pakistan and Sri Lanka expressed their deep appreciation for the exemplary manner in which the President of the Maldives had discharged his responsibilities as Chairman of the Meeting. They expressed their profound gratitude for the warm and gracious hospitality extended to them by the Government and the people of the Maldives

and for the excellent arrangements made for the Meeting.

Joint Press Release

Joint Press Release issued on 23 November 1990 at the end of the Fifth SAARC Summit, Male'.

1. The President of Bangladesh, the King of Bhutan, the Prime Minister of India, the President of the Maldives, the Prime Minister of Nepal, the Prime Minister of Pakistan and the Prime Minister of Sri Lanka met at the Fifth Summit of the South Asian Association for Regional Cooperation at Male' from 21-23 November 1990. The Meeting was held in an atmosphere of warmth, cordiality and mutual understanding.

2. The Heads of State or Government reaffirmed their commitment to the principles and objectives of SAARC and reiterated their resolve to intensify cooperation under its aegis. They issued the Male' Declaration.

3. They welcomed the signing of the SAARC Convention on Narcotic Drugs and Psychotropic Substances by the Ministers at Male' and undertook to take early measures to ratify the Convention.

4. The Heads of State or Government decided to launch the Special SAARC Travel Document which would exempt its holders from visas for travel within the region. They decided that Supreme Court Judges, Members of the National Parliaments, Heads of national academic institutions, their spouses and dependent children would be entitled to this Document.

5. The Heads of State or Government endorsed the decision of the Council of Ministers to launch the Scheme for the Promotion of Organised Tourism during the first half of 1991. They also welcomed the proposal for institutionalised cooperation among the tourist industries of the Member States with a view to attracting more tourists from outside the region.

6. They noted with satisfaction that all Member States had completed their national studies on Trade, Manufactures and Services. They underlined the need for completing the Regional Study within the stipulated timeframe.

7. They decided that measures for establishing joint ventures in the field of cottage industries and handicrafts should be taken up forthwith to set a stage for promoting collective selfreliance in the region. They directed the SecretaryGeneral to appoint a group of 23 Experts selected from within the region, to prepare a paper suggesting the modalities for the setting up of joint ventures, sources of funding and other necessary details for consideration at the next meeting of the Council of Ministers.

8. The Heads of State or Government noted the proposal for the establishment of a SAARC Regional Fund and directed the Standing Committee to submit its recommendations on the proposal for consideration at the next session of the Council of Ministers.

9. The Heads of State or Government emphasized the importance of cooperation among the SAARC Member States in the field of mass media and directed the SecretaryGeneral to facilitate, under the auspices of SAARC,increased interaction among federations/

associations of journalists, news agencies and mass media of the region.

10. The Heads of State or Government welcomed the decision authorizing the Secretariat to share information and exchange reports, studies and publications with the European Community (EC) and the Association of South East Asian Nations (ASEAN), to begin with, in the identified areas of cooperation.

11. The Heads of State or Government expressed satisfaction that the work was well under way for the setting up of a nucleus Centre for Human Resource Development in Pakistan. They were of the view that the Centre would contribute towards optimizing regional cooperation in this vital field.

12. They called for early completion of a regional plan "SAARC 2000 A Basic Needs Perspective" to facilitate activities within a broad framework of a long term perspective.

13. They directed that the theme of 'Poverty Alleviation' Strategies be discussed in depth by Planners for formulating suitable recommendations.

14. The Heads of State or Government decided that in order to maintain focus on the problems of the Girl Child the years 19912000 AD would be observed as the "SAARC Decade of the Girl Child". They were deeply moved by the SAARC Girl Child's appeal for love and care for them and their right to childhood. They reiterated their resolve that the welfare of the child in general and the girl child in particular, would figure at the top of their list of priorities.

15. The Heads of State or Government emphasized the importance of regular exchange of views among the

representatives of the SAARC Member Countries at international economic fora with a view to concerting positions, as far as possible, on matters of common concern. They decided to hold the Second Ministerial Meeting on International Economic Issues in India in 1991.

16. The Heads of State or Government underlined the imperative need for providing a better habitat to the people of South Asia and decided that in order to focus attention on the problems of the Homeless, the Year 1991 be observed as the "SAARC Year of Shelter". They decided that each country would organise a series of events on this theme and share their experiences in order that the people of the region could derive practical benefit from the "SAARC Year of Shelter".

17. They directed that the Regional Study on the Causes and Consequences of Natural Disasters and the Protection and Preservation of the Environment and the Study on the 'Greenhouse Effect' and its impact on the region be finalized before the next Summit. They stressed that, pending the completion of the studies, Member States should take necessary steps at national levels in this vital field. They decided to observe 1992 as the "SAARC Year of the Environment".

18. The Heads of State or Government stressed that immediate action was required to reduce the sufferings of the millions of disabled people who lived in the SAARC region. In order to focus attention on their problems and to improve their quality of life, they decided to observe 1993 as the "SAARC Year of Disabled Persons".

19. They decided that appropriate programmes should be worked out for observing the SAARC Year of the Shelter 1991, the SAARC Year of the Environment 1992, and the SAARC Year of Disabled Persons 1993. In order to derive the maximum benefit and to sensitize the peoples in the region in the above vital fields, they noted that Sri Lanka, the Maldives and Pakistan respectively will circulate the recommended Plans of Action for implementation at national level.

20. The Heads of State or Government noted that SAARC Agricultural Information Centre (SAIC) was already functioning at Dhaka. They decided that the SAARC Tuberculosis Centre and the SAARC Documentation Centre would be set up in Nepal and India respectively. They directed that necessary steps to establish the two Centres should be taken up urgently.

21. The Heads of State or Government stressed the need for adopting a more businesslike and functional approach in the conduct of meetings held under the aegis of SAARC. They requested the Chairman of the Fifth SAARC Summit and the President of Bangladesh to initiate consultations with the Member States in this regard.

22. The Heads of State or Government directed the Chairman of Council of Ministers to prepare recommendations on rationalizing SAARC activities with a view to promoting effective functioning of the Association.

23. The Heads of State or Government expressed appreciation for the pioneering work done by Ambassador Abul Ahsan, the first SecretaryGeneral, during the formative years of the Secretariat. They welcomed his successor, Ambassador Kant Kishore

Bhargava, and appreciated his valuable contribution to the ongoing activities of SAARC.

24. They expressed profound happiness that the Fifth SAARC Summit coincided with the TwentyFifth Anniversary of the Independence of the Maldives which provided them with an opportunity to express personally their solidarity with the people and the Government of the Maldives.

25. The Heads of State or Government gratefully accepted the offer of the Government of Sri Lanka to host the Sixth SAARC Summit in Colombo in 1991.

26. The Heads of State or Government highly appreciated the exemplary manner in which the President of the Republic of Maldives conducted the meetings of the Association as the Chairman of the Fifth SAARC Summit. They also expressed their sincere gratitude for the gracious hospitality extended to them by the Government and the people of the Republic of Maldives and for the excellent arrangements made for the Conference.

9

Declaration of the Sixth SAARC Summit, Colombo

The Colombo Declaration of the Heads of State or Government of the Member Countries of South Asian Association for Regional Cooperation issued on 21st December 1991.

Introduction

1. The Prime Minister of the People's Republic of Bangladesh, Her Excellency Begum Khaleda Zia; the King of Bhutan, His Majesty King Jigme Singye Wangchuck; the Prime Minister of the Republic of India, His Excellency Shri Narasimha Rao; the President of the Republic of Maldives, His Excellency Mr. Maumoon Abdul Gayoom; the Prime Minister of Nepal, the Rt. Hon. Girija Prasad Koirala; the Prime Minister of the Islamic Republic of Pakistan, His Excellency Mian Mohammed Nawaz Sharif and the President of the Democratic Socialist Republic of Sri Lanka, His Excellency Ranasinghe Premadasa met at

the Sixth Summit of the South Asian Association for Regional Cooperation (SAARC) at Colombo, Sri Lanka on 21st December, 1991.

2. The Heads of State or Government reaffirmed their commitment to the principles and objectives enshrined in the Charter of SAARC. They resolved to promote regional cooperation for the benefit of their people, in a spirit of mutual accommodation, with full respect for the principles of sovereign equality, independence and territorial integrity of all States and in strict adherence to the principles of nonuse of force, the peaceful settlement of disputes and noninterference in each other's internal affairs. They also reiterated their commitment to the principles of the United Nations Charter and the Nonaligned Movement.

3. The Heads of State or Government emphasised the vital importance of assessing the nature and extent of international economic interdependence and of the need for reviving the North/South dialogue. They noted the recent developments that had radically transformed the international development relationship deeply affecting the prospects for the economies of the seven SAARC countries. The Heads of State or Government emphasised the need for vigorously promoting SouthSouth economic cooperation to offset the negative consequences of international economic developments.

4. The Heads of State or Government also exchanged views on the priorities of their respective national economies. They identified, for the further development of their economies, the importance of securing less restrictive trading and marketing

opportunities for their products, more extensive technology and resource transfers to South Asia, debt relief and access on favourable and on more concessional terms to resources from multilateral financial institutions. They agreed to keep an open dialogue on these aspects through mutual consultations.

5. The Heads of State or Government assessed current international developments in the political sphere particularly those that affected the lives of the people of South Asia. They noted the changing power structures in international relations and the reduction of confrontations and tensions, particularly among the Super Powers. These have contributed to the receding of the threat of nuclear confrontation and to agreements on disarmament measures. The Heads of State or Government hoped that these developments would restrain the pursuit of military power in all areas of the world. They expressed the hope that the peace dividend would be used for promoting further development of developing countries. They welcomed the trend towards popularly based democratic governments in different parts of the world including in South Asia.

6. The Heads of State or Government observed however that some political issues in particular the Palestine question, the final elimination of Apartheid as well as other problems remained unresolved despite efforts towards their settlement.

7. In regard to human rights, the Heads of State or Government observed that civil and political rights on the one hand and economic and social rights on the other are interdependent and of equal importance

Human rights issues should not therefore be viewed in narrow and exclusively political terms. In this context they underlined the need to view the efforts of States to guarantee human rights in their full context, through the pursuit of development for all citizens in conditions of stability, which in turn guarantees the enjoyment of human rights of all persons.

8. The Heads of State or Government while reaffirming their commitment to democracy, human rights and the rule of law, emphasised the need to ensure that development remains at the centre of international attention.

9. The Heads of State or Government agreed to participate in the ongoing process of revitalising the United Nations as an effective universal instrument for addressing international issues on an equitable and democratic basis, taking full account of the interests and concerns of all states, including those in South Asia. Issues such as the protection and preservation of the environment and the equitable and sustainable management of global resources, economic development and the alleviation of poverty, the suppression of terrorism, drug trafficking and other international crimes required global responses and solutions calling for action by all states.

10. In the context of the SAARC Charterobjective to strengthen cooperation among MemberStates in international fora, the Heads of State or Government resolved to encourage consultations among delegations of SAARC countries at all international fora and to promote articulation of joint positions

where such action would be in the interests of all. They felt that the development of a collective position in international fora would accord them greater credibility and enhance the international profile of South Asia.

11. The Heads of State or Government welcomed the Report presented by the Chairman of the Fifth SAARC Summit, the President of Maldives, and the Head of Government of Bangladesh on the adoption of a more businesslike and functional approach in the conduct of SAARC meetings, as well as the Report submitted by the Chairman of the Ninth Session of the Council of Ministers, the Foreign Minister of Maldives, on rationalizing SAARC activities. The Heads of State or Government also considered other proposals submitted by MemberStates and by the Secretariat to make the Association a more effective instrument for the realisation of the aspirations of the people of South Asia.

12. They decided that the Standing Committee should meet in special session in Colombo in April 1992 in order to collate and study all proposals and comments in this respect and to submit a report with its recommendations to the Eleventh Session of the Council of Ministers.

13. The Heads of State or Government reemphasised that regional selfreliance should be resolutely promoted through closer cooperation among countries of the Association and that this would help mitigate the adverse consequences of negative international developments operating against them.

14. The Heads of State or Government requested the Standing Committee at its Special Session to study

the question of cooperation between SAARC and appropriate international and regional organizations taking into account the evolution of SAARC activities in the core economic areas and to report to the Eleventh Session of the Council of Ministers.

15. The Heads of State or Government noted the progress made by the Integrated Programme of Action (IPA) in expanding to cover a number of sectors crucial for the economic and social progress of the peoples of South Asia. They were of the view that the challenge facing the IPA was to achieve its identified targets within specific time periods. The Heads of State or Government welcomed the proposals made and the discussions proceeding in SAARC to heighten the effectiveness of the IPA.

16. The Heads of State or Government accorded the highest priority to the alleviation of poverty in all South Asian countries. They affirmed that South Asia's poor could constitute a huge and potential resource, provided their basic needs were met, and they were mobilized to create economic growth. This requires that the poor are empowered and are irreversibly linked to the mainstream of development. It was noted that each South Asian country has had significant success cases of this approach to poverty alleviation.

17. Recognising that a great majority of these people remain below the poverty line, they evinced keen interest in a "Daal-Bhaat", or assured nutritional standards approach towards the satisfaction of basic needs of the South Asian poor.

18. Deeply conscious that primary education is the cutting edge in the struggle against poverty and the

promotion of development, the Heads of State or Government reaffirmed the importance of attaining the target of providing primary education to all children between the ages of 6 14 years by the year 2000. They agreed to share their respective experiences and technical expertise to achieve this goal.

19. The Heads of State or Government decided to establish an independent South Asian Commission on Poverty Alleviation consisting of eminent persons from each SAARC Member State to conduct an indepth study of diverse experiences of the seven countries on poverty alleviation, and to report to the Seventh Summit, their recommendations on the alleviation of poverty in South Asia.

20. The Heads of State or Government were pleased to note the establishment of the Committee for Economic Cooperation as an important outcome of the Regional Study on Trade Manufactures and Services. They declared their commitment to the liberalisation of trade in the region through a step by step approach in such a manner that all countries in the region share the benefits of trade expansion equitably.

21. The Heads of State or Government approved that the Inter Governmental Group (IGG) set up on the recommendation of the Committee on Economic Cooperation should formulate and seek agreement on an institutional framework under which specific measures for trade liberalisation among SAARC Member States could be furthered. It should also examine the Sri Lankan proposal to establish a SAARC Preferential Trade Arrangement (SAPTA) by

1997. They directed that the IGG should meet as early as possible and report to the Committee on Economic Cooperation. The Heads of State or Government accepted the offer of the Government of Sri Lanka to host the Second Meeting of the Committee on Economic Cooperation at Colombo in June/July 1992 at which the report of the Inter Governmental Group would be considered.

22. The Heads of State or Government recognised that the degradation of the environment has emerged as a major global concern. While the protection of the environment is a common imperative for all humankind, the main responsibility in this regard rests on developed countries since most of the emission of pollutants originates in those countries and since they also have greater capacity for taking or facilitating corrective measures.

23. The Heads of State or Government called on the international community to address the question of unsustainable production and consumption patterns and lifestyles which lead to environmental degradation. They were also of the view that environmental standards applicable to developed countries may have excessive and unwarranted economic or social costs if applied in developing countries.

24. Adequate new and additional resources are needed for developing countries to pursue an environmentally sensitive process of development that will banish the underlying causes of environmental degradation poverty, malnutrition and unemployment. Such resources should be transferred to developing countries on an assured basis together

with environmentally sound technology at preferential and concessional terms.

25. The Heads of State or Government expressed their conviction that the framework could be laid for an equitable global partnership of all countries with a view to safeguarding the environment.

26. The Heads of State or Government noted that in preparation for the SAARC Year of the Environment, SAARC countries had taken various national as well as regional measures for the preservation of the environment.

27. The Heads of State or Government expressed their satisfaction at the completion of Regional Study on the Causes and Consequences of Natural Disasters and the Protection and Preservation of Environment. They urged the member countries to promote cooperation amongst themselves for enhancing their respective disaster management capabilities and for undertaking specific workprogrammes for protection and preservation of the environment.

    They endorsed the decision of the Council of Ministers to establish a Committee on Environment to:

    — examine the recommendations of the Regional Study

    — identify measures for immediate action

    — decide on modalities for their implementation and welcomed the offer of Bangladesh to hold the first meeting of the Committee in Dhaka.

28. The Heads of State or Government noted with satisfaction the decision of the Standing Committee

concerning the time frame to finalise the regional study on the " 'Greenhouse Effect' and its Impact on the Region". They urged member countries to consult each other on key issues concerning climate change, Biodiversity and Biotechnology, a global consensus on forestry principles, transfer of environmentally sound technology, management of waste and other issues for discussion at Intergovernmental Negotiating Committee and the UNCED in 1992 so that the concerns of SAARC countries could be effectively articulated and projected, keeping in mind their respective national priorities.

29. The Government of India renewed its offer to host a Ministerial Meeting to harmonise the views of SAARC countries on these issues before UNCED 1992. The Heads of State or Government welcomed the offer.

30. The Heads of State or Government noted the useful activities conducted during 1991 which was observed as SAARC Year of Shelter. They decided to continue to work towards the global objective of "Shelter for All by the Year 2000.

31. The Heads of State or Government were of the view that Governments should play the critical role of facilitator and supporter of the initiatives of the people and nongovernmental agencies in the field of shelter. In this role, they should be involved in the provision of affordable sites with secure tenure, making housing finance available on an affordable and sustainable basis, providing infrastructure development such as water supply and sanitation, energy and waste disposal, increasing the supply of building materials at reasonable prices using

indigenous resources, removing constraints to building activities, and creating maximum opportunities for public participation in decision making and management of shelter activities in the overall context of poverty alleviation. Such activities would be facilitated by the exchange of experience, personnel, research and information among the SAARC countries.

32. The Heads of State or Government welcomed the recommendation on the establishment of a shelter information network to be called "SHELTERNET".

33. The Heads of State or Government accorded the highest priority to the question of child survival, protection and development. They welcomed the adoption of a Plan of Action on Children for South Asia which incorporated relevant recommendations of the World Summit on Children.

34. The Heads of State or Government noted in this context that some member countries had completed their national Plans of Action and urged other member countries to complete their respective Plans. They also urged Member States to ensure coordinated followup action on their respective Plans.

35. The Heads of State or Government welcomed the offer of Sri Lanka to host a Conference on Children in South Asia in 1992 to consider implementation of the regional Plan of Action.

36. The Heads of State or Government welcomed the adoption of the Plan of Action for 1991 2000 A.D. as the SAARC Decade of the Girl Child. They requested the Council of Ministers to ensure an annual review of the status of implementation of the Plan of Action during the decade.

37. The Heads of State or Government expressed serious concern on the spread of terrorism in the region affecting the security and stability of all Member States and unequivocally condemned all acts, methods and practices of terrorism as criminal. They deplored all such acts for their impact on life, property, socio-economic development and political stability as well as on regional and international peace and cooperation.

38. They recognised that cooperation among SAARC States was vital if terrorism was to be prevented and eliminated from the region. In this regard they urged Member States to take all necessary measures to give full effect to their obligations under the SAARC Regional Convention on Suppression of Terrorism. They stressed in particular, the urgent need for the expeditious enactment of enabling legislation by those Member States which had not yet done so, for the implementation of the Convention and the need for a constant dialogue and interaction among the concerned agencies of Member States, including submission of periodic recommendations to the Council of Ministers.

39. The Heads of State or Government welcomed the initiative of the Government of the Republic of Maldives in drawing the attention of the international community to the protection and security of small states. They noted with satisfaction that the resolution submitted by the Maldives to the United Nations during the 46th Session of the General Assembly and cosponsored by 65 countries including all the members of SAARC was adopted without a vote. They agreed that small states may be particularly vulnerable to external threats and acts of

interference in their internal affairs and that they merit special measures of support in safeguarding their sovereign independence, territorial integrity and the welfare of their people.

40. The Heads of State or Government noted with satisfaction the increasing regional cooperation in combating the problem of drug trafficking and drug abuse. They expressed serious concern over the growing linkages between drug trafficking, international arms trade and terrorist activities. While expressing satisfaction at the signing of the SAARC Convention on Narcotic Drugs and Psychotropic Substances at the Fifth SAARC Summit at Malé, they urged Member States which had not yet done so to ratify the Convention for its entry into force. They also recognised the need for greater cooperation, including the submission of periodic recommendations to the Council of Ministers.

41. The Heads of State or Government recalled that important initiatives had been taken at the Bangalore and Kathmandu Summits which had subsequently resulted in the increased involvement of the peoples of South Asia in the process of Regional Cooperation. They welcomed the steps being taken by business organisations/ professional bodies, scholars, academics, National Cultural Councils and the media in South Asia to form regional entities/ bodies. They called on the Standing Committee to expedite the formulation of guidelines for extending recognition to such groups and bodies.

42. The Heads of State or Government welcomed the setting up of a SAARC Fund for Regional Projects (SFRP) for identification and development of regional

projects. They noted that the Fund would be managed by a Regional Council of Development Financing Institutions of the SAARC Member States and that the First Meeting of the Council would take place in India.

43. The Heads of State or Government requested the Secretary-General of SAARC to set up a panel of experts to examine the proposal of His Majesty the King of Bhutan to undertake a prefeasibility study for the establishment of a South Asian Development Fund, taking into account the views of all Member States.

44. The Heads of State or Government noted with satisfaction that the Scheme in regard to the entitled categories of Members of Parliament, Judges of the Supreme Court, Heads of national academic institutions and the accompanying spouses and dependent children will become operational from 1st March 1992. They called for expeditious action to implement the scheme as well as to consider other categories eligible for exemption.

45. The Heads of State or Government were conscious of the vast potential being afforded by current advances in scientific research for the application of science and technology towards the wellbeing of the peoples of South Asia. They agreed that for the South Asian region to derive the maximum benefit, scientific and technological cooperation should transcend national frontiers.

46. Recalling the decision of the Malé Summit to institutionalise cooperation in the field of biotechnology, they welcomed the proposal for the establishment of a networking arrangement between

Research and Development Centres in the Member States as an important step in advancing such cooperation. They also welcomed the emphasis on organised study tours, workshops and seminars proposed in the identified areas of cooperation in the field of science and technology.

47. The Heads of State or Government gratefully accepted the offer of the Government of Bangladesh to host the Seventh SAARC Summit in 1992.

48. The Heads of State or Government of Bangladesh, Bhutan, India, Maldives, Nepal and Pakistan expressed their deep appreciation for the exemplary manner in which the President of Sri Lanka had discharged his responsibilities as Chairman of the Meeting. They expressed their profound gratitude for the warm and gracious hospitality extended to them by the Government and the people of Sri Lanka and for the excellent arrangements made for the Meeting.

10

Declaration of the Seventh SAARC Summit, Dhaka

The Declaration of the Seventh SAARC Summit of the Heads of State or Government of Member Countries of the South Asian Association for Regional Cooperation issued on 11th April 1993.

Introduction

1. The Prime Minister of the People's Republic of Bangladesh, Her Excellency Begum Khaleda Zia, the King of Bhutan, His Majesty Jigme Singye Wangchuck, the Prime Minister of the Republic of India, His Excellency Mr. P. V. Narasimha Rao, the President of the Republic of Maldives, His Excellency Mr. Maumoon Abdul Gayoom, the Prime Minister of Nepal, the Rt. Hon. Girija Prasad Koirala, the Prime Minister of the Islamic Republic of Pakistan, His Excellency Mr. Mohammed Nawaz Sharif and the President of the Democratic Socialist Republic of Shri Lanka, His Excellency Mr. Ranasinghe Premadasa

met at the Seventh Summit of the South Asian Association for Regional Cooperation (SAARC) at Dhaka, Bangladesh on 10 - 11 April, 1993.

Regional Cooperation

2. The Heads of State or Government reiterated their commitment to the principles and objectives of the South Asian Association for Regional Cooperation (SAARC), to the five principles of peaceful co-existence, the UN Charter and non-alignment. The Heads of State or Government noted the progress achieved in regional cooperation under the aegis of SAARC. They felt that time was now opportune for SAARC to provide a further dynamic impetus to activities in the core areas of economic, social and cultural cooperation in the SAARC region.

Integrated Programme of Action (IPA)

3. The Heads of State or Government welcomed the recent specific steps taken to consolidate and further streamline IPA-related SAARC activities. They also stressed the need for a progressive movement towards undertaking more well-defined, target-oriented and time- bound projects and programmes to ensure tangible benefits for the peoples of South Asia.

Activities Outside IPA

4. The Leaders welcomed the recent decisions to institutionalize cooperation in the core areas.

More Business-Like and Functional Approache in the Conduct of SAARC Meetings

5. The Heads of State or Government approved the recommendations of the Eleventh Session of the Council of Ministers for adopting a more business-like and functional approach in the conduct of Summit meetings. They also noted with satisfaction the guidelines and procedures approved by the Eleventh Session of the Council in this respect relating to other SAARC meetings. They decided to meet informally whenever necessary, between Summits.

Consensus on Eradication of Poverty in South Asia

6. Conscious that the sheer magnitude and complexity of South Asian poverty constituted a major political and economic challenge, the Heads of State or Government reiterated their commitment to continue to accord a high priority to its eradication from the region in the shortest possible time.

7. They pledged to overcome this challenge through the implementation of appropriate pro-poor development strategies at macro and micro levels.

8. In this context, the Heads of State or Government welcomed the Report of the Independent South Asian Commission on Poverty Alleviation established at the Colombo Summit. The Report provided valuable insight and illustrative examples of successful poverty alleviation programmes in individual Member States.

9. Acknowledging that the abiding human qualities of dignity, creativity and productive potential are eroded by chronic poverty, the Heads of State or Government reiterated their commitment to empowering the poor for enhanced growth, consistent with human development and equity.

10. The Heads of State or Government committed their Governments unequivocally to the eradication of poverty in South Asia, preferably by the year 2002 A.D. through an Agenda of Action, which would, inter-alia, embody :

    -A strategy of social mobilization involving the building of organizations of the poor and their empowerment through appropriate national support mechanisms, with the assistance of respective Governments;

    - A policy of decentralized agricultural development and sharply focussed household level food security through universal provision of 'Daal-Bhaat' or basic nutritional needs;

    - A policy of decentralized small scale labour intensive industrialization, with the choice of efficient and cost-effective technology;

    - A policy of human development, including the enhancement of the social role and status of poor women, the provision of universal primary education, skill development, primary health care, shelter for the poor and protection of children; - A policy to support the above initiatives with adequate financial resources.

11. The Heads of State or Government stressed that within the overall conceptual approach of 'Daal-

Bhaat', the right to work and the right to primary education should receive priority.

12. The Leaders also underscored the critical link between the success of national efforts aimed at poverty alleviation and the external factors affecting growth and development. They urged all major actors in the world economic scene, particularly the industrialized countries and multilateral and regional financial institutions, and Non-Governmental Organizations to create an enabling international atmosphere that is supportive of poverty alleviation programmes in South Asia. This would require a new dialogue with donors.

13. The Heads of State or Government agreed to the follow-up action indicated below :

    - a national level pro-poor plan to be drawn up by each Member State. This plan is to be harmonized with the open economy and structural adjustment strategies;
    - to share during the next Summit, information regarding the progress achieved.

Trade, Manufacures and Services

14. The Heads of State or Government reaffirmed the need to liberalize trade as early as possible through a step by step approach. They underscored that this should be done in such a manner that all countries in the region could share the benefits of trade expansion equitably.

15. In this context, the Heads of State or Government welcomed the finalization of the framework

Agreement on SAARC Preferential Trading Arrangement (SAPTA). They expressed their deep satisfaction over the signing of the framework Agreement. The Leaders stressed that all necessary steps should be taken to begin the first round of trade negotiations to exchange trade preferences among Member States under the Arrangement.

16. The Heads of State or Government further underlined the critical importance of urgently promoting intra-regional cooperation, particularly in the area of manufactures in order to enhance the productive capacity of the Member Countries, and to promote sustained growth and development to prevent the marginalization of South Asia's trade interest in the larger global context.

Environment

17. The Heads of State or Government expressed their deep concern at the unabated degradation of the environment and recurrence of devastating natural disasters. They also underscored the risks and dangers involved in overlooking the challenge posed by these problems. They expressed their commitment to implementing at all levels - national, bilateral, regional and global - programmes for the protection and preservation of the environment and prevention of its degradation. The Heads of State or Government recognized that the completion of the Regional Study on the "`Greenhouse Effect' and its Impact on the Region" was a significant step forward in promoting regional cooperation in this vital area. They also stressed the importance of continuing the ongoing SAARC activities in the field of environment.

18. The Heads of State or Government welcomed the outcome of the United Nations Conference on Environment and Development held in Rio de Janeiro in 1992 and underscored the imperative need to ensure the flow of resources to successfully implement the wide range of suggested initiatives and actions contained in Agenda 21. The Heads of State or Government noted that all international actions in the area of environment should be based on common but differential responsibilities, collective endeavours and a balanced perspective. Such actions, they stressed, must consider the protection of environment, economic growth and eradication of poverty as mutually reinforcing. All environmental initiatives, they underscored, must preclude the imposition of arbitrary and one-sided pre-conditions and ensure a harmonious blending of environmental and development concerns. They further noted with satisfaction the establishment of the Commission on Sustainable Development. They urged that the Commission approach environmental problems of developed and developing countries in an equitable manner.

19. The Heads of State or Government expressed their satisfaction over the adoption of a common position by Member States prior to the United Nations Conference on Environment and Development. They expressed their determination to continue in future the practice of intra-SAARC consultations on matters of common concern.

Population

20. Recognizing the sovereign right of all countries to promote, adopt and implement their population

policies and mindful of their cultures, values and traditions, the Heads of State or Government stressed the need to integrate demographic objectives and population strategies in the formulation of the development strategies of Member Countries. In this context, they also noted the importance of adequate investment in the health and education sectors for the success of their population programmes. They agreed that cooperation among Member States should be strengthened, both through sharing experiences and in other practical ways, to enhance their capacity to deal with the population problem. The Leaders urged Governments of developed countries, as well as all concerned international and regional organizations, to strengthen their financial and technical support in the areas of health and education as part of their strategy of assistance to developing countries in their development efforts.

21. The Heads of State or Government welcomed the offer of Nepal to host a SAARC Ministerial Conference on Women and Family Health in Kathmandu in October/November 1993.

Shelter

22. The Heads of State or Government reiterated that housing was a basic right for all people and that Governments should act as facilitator and supporter of shelter programmes initiated by the people. They urged Member States to continue to work towards the global objective of "Shelter for All by the Year 2000".

Children

23. Reaffirming their commitment to accord the highest priority to child survival, protection and development, the Heads of State or Government noted with satisfaction that all Member States had completed their National Plans of Action on Children. They reiterated their call at the Colombo Summit to continue to ensure coordinated follow-up action by Member States on their respective plans.

24. The Heads of State or Government endorsed the "Colombo Resolution on Children" adopted by the Second SAARC Ministerial Conference on Children held at Colombo in September 1992 and urged Member States to implement programmes as appropriate in their respective national contexts, to achieve the illustrative goals embodied in the Resolution, and the goals of the SAARC Plan of Action on Children.

25. The Heads of State or Government noted, in particular, the need to take effective measures to protect children against all forms of neglect, cruelty and exploitation and agreed to promote cooperation among Member States in devising such measures.

Youth

26. Stressing that the youth of South Asia constituted a vital resource for national development and that mobilization of their latent power was imperative, the Heads of State or Government focussed special attention on the needs of the Youth in South Asia and their development.

27. The Leaders noted that the youth of South Asia faced a number of serious problems requiring urgent attention and remedial measures. They welcomed the offer of the Maldives to host a Ministerial Conference on Youth in South Asia in 1994 to address the problems of the Youth and focus on the broad theme of youth and development. They also agreed to designate 1994 as the "SAARC Year of the Youth".

Plan of Action for the Disables Persons

28. The Heads of State or Government while recalling their decision at the Male' Summit to observe 1993 as the "SAARC Year of Disabled Persons", adopted the Regional Plan of Action for the Disabled Persons. They urged Member States to take concrete steps to implement the Plan.

29. They welcomed the offer of Pakistan to host a Ministerial Conference on Disabled Persons in September 1993.

Women in Development

30. While reviewing the situation of women in the region, it was noted with satisfaction that over a period of time, the content of regional cooperation which addresses the issue of development, gender and equality for women has steadily grown in SAARC. The Heads of State or Government hoped that the cooperation thus developed will enable Member States to achieve the ultimate goal of bringing women into the mainstream of development with independence and equality.

31. The Heads of State or Government recalled that in pursuance of their collective will expressed in the Male' Summit to observe the 1990s as the " SAARC Decade of the Girl Child", Member States had undertaken to formulate National Plans of Action for the improvement of the condition of the Girl Child giving priority to her survival, protection and development. They expressed satisfaction that some Member States had already completed this task and others were expected to do so soon.

Sceince and Technology

32. The Heads of State or Government emphasized that cooperation in the field of Science and Technology was of utmost importance in order to accelerate the process of development in South Asia.

33. They called for further intensification of efforts by Member States in this important area, particularly to facilitate research and exchange of information through networking arrangements in the field of bio-technology, genetic engineering, energy modelling techniques and other identified areas of cooperation.

Terrorism

34. The Heads of State or Government reiterated their unequivocal condemnation of all acts, methods and practices of terrorism as criminal. They strongly deplored the adverse consequences of terrorism.

35. They noted with grave concern that the efforts to combat the growing threat of terrorism had resulted

in the diversion of valuable scarce resources from urgent development programmes.

36. The Leaders reiterated the need to give high priority to the enactment of enabling legislation at the national level to give effect to the SAARC Regional Convention on Suppression of Terrorism, while urging the Member States which had not yet done so, to make every effort to finalize this matter before the Eighth SAARC Summit.

37. While recognizing that some progress had been achieved in the fields of consultation and exchange of information, they stressed the need for further enhancing cooperation in these fields as well as for coordinated action. They called for the expeditious implementation of the recommendations formulated for advancing cooperation in this regard in pursuance of their decision at the Colombo Summit.

Drug Trafficking and Drug Abuse

38. The Heads of State or Government reiterated their grave concern at the growing menace of drug trafficking in the region and the aggravation of the problem of drug abuse among the South Asian population, particularly the youth.

39. They recognized the devastating impact of drug abuse on the very fabric of society and the serious threat to security and stability posed by drug trafficking through its growing linkages with organized crime, illicit arms trade and terrorism.

40. The Heads of State or Government were gratified to note the expanding cooperation among Member

States to combat and eliminate the scourge of drug trafficking and drug abuse.

41. They reiterated the need for further strengthening cooperation in this field and called for the expeditious implementation of the recommendations formulated for this purpose in pursuance of their decision at the Colombo Summit.

Security of Small States

42. The Heads of State or Government reaffirmed their commitment to pay special attention to the monitoring of the security of small States and underscored the need to consider special measures of support to preserve their sovereign independence, territorial integrity and the well-being of their people. They further noted that real protection of small and weaker States should be firmly rooted in the Rule of Law and strict adherence to universally accepted principles and norms relating to the sovereign rights and territorial integrity of all States - big or small. This, they stressed, should be ensured by all countries either severally or collectively through the pursuit of appropriate actions.

People-to-People Contact

43. The Heads of State or Government stressed the need to further promote people-to-people contact in order to ensure increased involvement of peoples of South Asia in the process of regional cooperation. In this context, they noted that the formulation of guidelines and procedures for extending recognition to regional

apex bodies would facilitate participation of these bodies in promoting regional cooperation at the people-to-people level.

44. The Leaders expressed the hope that the recent recognition of the SAARC Chamber of Commerce and Industry would contribute positively to enhancing cooperation in the crucial areas of trade and economic relations.

45. The Heads of State or Government expressed their appreciation to the Government and people of India for hosting the First South Asian Festival of SAARC Countries in 1992. The Festival provided the people of the region the opportunity to share in the rich cultural heritage of South Asia. The Heads of State or Government hoped that the South Asian Festival would become a regular feature.

Association of SAARC Speakers and Parlimentarians

46. The Heads of State or Government welcomed the initiative of the Speakers of Parliaments of SAARC Countries in forming an "Association of SAARC Speakers and Parliamentarians". They were of the view that the establishment of this Association would add another important dimension to the process of regional cooperation.

South Asian Development Fund

47. The Heads of State or Government endorsed the recommendation of the Council of Ministers for the establishment of an Inter-Governmental Group (IGG)

on South Asian Development Fund (SADF) on an ad-hoc basis. They directed that the IGG define in clear terms the size, structure, resources and operational modalities of the proposed Fund. They also directed the IGG to examine the complementarities between the SAARC Fund for Regional Projects (SFRP) and SADF, and their relationship, including the possibility of their merger. They welcomed the offer of the Maldives to host the meeting of IGG.

International Political Developments

48. The Heads of State or Government had wide-ranging discussions on the current global political trends and future prospects, particularly those issues that affect South Asia. In this context, they reiterated their deep commitment to the purposes and principles of the UN Charter and reaffirmed their resolve to strengthen the United Nations as the central instrument for peace, security, disarmament, development and cooperation among the nations of the world. To this end, the Leaders supported all constructive initiatives aimed at strengthening the United Nations. They, however, underscored that any move to adapt or reform the United Nations must be undertaken with the sole objective of rendering the United Nations more democratic, efficient and effective and not to limit the focus of its attention to a narrow and isolated range of objectives.

49. The Heads of State or Government reiterated their firm commitment to the principles and objectives of the Non-aligned Movement and underlined the continued validity and relevance of these principles

and objectives in the contemporary global political and economic context. They recalled the important role the Movement had been playing in strengthening international peace, promoting development and establishing more equitable and just economic relations and enhancing international cooperation in all areas. They expressed their deep conviction that the Movement's innate strength uniquely equipped it to continue to play a most constructive role in laying the foundations and defining the characteristics of a new world order which should be based on the principles of justice, equity and democracy in international relations. In this context, the Heads of State or Government welcomed the success of the Jakarta Summit of the Non-aligned countries and called for the expeditious implementation of its decisions.

50. The Heads of State or Government noted that the end of the cold war presented new opportunities and challenges. They observed that despite many positive developments and recent successes in resolving some regional conflicts, the international political scene was still marred by strife and tension. They expressed their serious concern over the unfortunate and tragic consequences of ethnic conflict and violence afflicting people and communities in many parts of the world. They stressed that efforts must be intensified to find peaceful and viable solutions to conflicts of long standing nature and new problems through greater respect for international law and universally accepted humanitarian norms and standards.

51. The Heads of State or Government noted a number of recent positive developments in the area of

nuclear, chemical and conventional disarmament including the agreements on bilateral arms reductions between the United States and the Russian Federation. They expressed their hope that the implementation of the far-reaching arms reduction agreed in the Washington Agreement of June 1992 and START II signed in Moscow in January 1993 would be successfully carried out. The Leaders urged all Nuclear-Weapon States to collectively endeavour to attain the ultimate goal of complete elimination of nuclear arsenals in the shortest possible time.

52. They also underscored the imperative to further broaden and deepen the dimensions to disarmament and to complement bilateral approaches to disarmament with effective multilateral approaches. While welcoming the recent progress in arms reduction at the global level, the Leaders were convinced that this objective could be best achieved through the promotion of mutual trust and confidence among Member States.

Internation Economic Issues

53. The Heads of State or Government noted that while it was important to build peace and create conditions of stability in the world, it was equally important to promote economic and social development. They underscored that international cooperation for development and eradication of poverty were inextricably linked with the preservation of international peace and security and hence needed to be treated on an equal footing and pursued with equal vigour. The Heads of State or Government expressed their grave concern over the continuing

deterioration in economic situation in the majority of developing countries. The economies of developing countries, they observed, continued to suffer as a result of limited market access for their exports, dwindling resource flows, absence of adequate foreign investment, mounting external indebtedness, inadequate transfer of technology and the inequities in the global monetary, financial and trading systems. The Heads of State or Government noted that although the developing countries themselves had the primary responsibility for their economic development, the role of developed countries remained central to the revival of the growth of the world economy - in particular the economies of the developing countries.

54. The Heads of State or Government reiterated the vital importance of economic interdependence among nations and of the need for reviving North-South dialogue. They fully endorsed the view that there should be more equitable economic opportunities for all nations. These should include such important features as the strengthening of a free, open and non-discriminatory multilateral trading system, effective macro-economic coordination and fiscal discipline to ensure stable conditions conducive to development in the global economy. They also reiterated their firm support for the broadening of the coordination of international macro-economic policies to take into account concerns of all countries, specially the developing countries. Referring to the competing demands for capital and investment resources, the Heads of State or Government underscored the need to ensure the adequate flow of investment resources to the developing countries through increasing global

savings and a more equitable utilization of the peace dividends. In this context the Heads of State or Government also underscored the need to fulfil the internationally agreed aid targets for the developing countries and the Least Developed Countries. They emphasized on the need for exceptional finance to facilitate implementation of economic reform programmes in SAARC Countries.

55. The Heads of State or Government also strongly underlined the need to continue efforts to seek a comprehensive, durable and growth-oriented solution to the external indebtedness of the developing countries. This, they stressed, was essential to accelerate the process of growth in these countries. A lasting solution to the debt crisis, the Heads of State or Government noted, must take into account the need to significantly reduce the stock and service of all types of debts of indebted developing countries to augment the concessional aid flows to SAARC Countries and work out anticipatory measures to prevent the recurrence and proliferation of the debt problem.

56. The Heads of State or Government also underlined the importance of a strengthened and liberalized international trading system. In this context, they noted that the successful conclusion of the Uruguay Round of Multilateral Trade Negotiations was a matter of great importance to the developing countries. Failure of the Round, the Leaders noted, would only further impair economic growth and encourage protectionist policy seriously weakening the multilateral trading system. The Heads of State or Government strongly urged the major partners in the Negotiations to demonstrate their political will and

take positive steps to ensure without further delay a satisfactory conclusion of the Uruguay Round. They further stressed that although the main thrust of these negotiations in the recent past had been in respect of new issues, there was an imperative need to ensure that the Uruguay Round fully take into account the concerns and interests of developing countries. This, the Heads of State or Government stressed, was particularly important. The Leaders underscored the need to speedily conclude the current round of negotiations in a transparent, balanced and expeditious manner. They also stressed that before the conclusion of the Uruguay Round of Multilateral Trade Negotiations, an evaluation of results be held from the point of view of developing countries.

57. The Heads of State or Government expressed their concern over the increasing stock of anti-dumping and countervailing duty investigations against the exports of developing countries and the new threats to a liberal trading order in the form of measures taken in pursuit of the goals relating to workers' rights and the environment.

Projections of Collective Positions

58. The Heads of State or Government were of the view that greater consultations among the delegations of SAARC Countries in all international fora on the major issues of common concern to them would be in the interest of all their countries. They felt that the development of collective positions on such issues in the international fora would enhance the

international profile of South Asia and would enable the countries in the region to articulate their position on them more effectively. They reiterated their common resolve to concert their position in all international fora and negotiations with a view to deriving maximum benefits from them in accordance with their needs and common priorities.

59. The Heads of State or Government underscored the vital importance attached by their countries to the forthcoming Second World Conference on Human Rights in 1993, the World Population Conference in 1994 and the 1995 World Conference on Women. They also supported the convening of a World Summit for Social Development. The Heads of State or Government stressed the need to develop a common South Asian perspective on the issues to be discussed by these important international conferences. They also underscored the imperative to coordinate the position of SAARC countries in order to ensure a balanced equitable and action oriented outcome of these conferences.

Observer Status

60. The Heads of State or Government decided that an Expert Group of the Member States will examine the various requests for observer status at SAARC/SAARC meetings in all its aspects on the basis of a working paper to be prepared by the Secretariat and make appropriate recommendations to the Nineteenth Session of the Standing Committee. In this respect, they welcomed the offer of Sri Lanka to host the Expert Group Meeting.

Conclusion

61. The Heads of State or Government expressed their deep satisfaction over the positive outcome of the Seventh SAARC Summit and expressed their conviction that this Summit would greatly contribute towards strengthening the policies and cooperative actions of the Member States in response to the challenges of the 1990s and beyond in areas where SAARC has a distinct contribution to make. They also reiterated once again their determination to strengthen and enrich SAARC as an instrument - endowing it with a clear set of forward looking goals and objectives as well as all the requisite institutional capacities - so that it can continue to work to enrich not only the lives of its own members but also promote peace, progress and stability in South Asia in a larger context.

Date and Venue of the Eighth Meeting of the SAARC Heads of State or Government

62. The Heads of State or Government gratefully accepted the offer of India to host the Eighth SAARC Summit in 1994.

63. The Heads of State or Government of Bhutan, India, the Maldives, Nepal, Pakistan and Sri Lanka expressed their sincere appreciation for the exemplary manner in which the Prime Minister of Bangladesh had conducted the Meeting and guided its proceedings in her capacity as Chairperson. They expressed their deep gratitude for the warm and generous hospitality extended to them by the Government and people of Bangladesh and for the excellent arrangements made for the Meeting.

11

Declaration of the Eighth SAARC Summit, New Delhi

The Delhi Declaration of the Heads of State or Government of the Member Countries of South Asian Association for Regional Cooperation issued on 4th May 1995.

Introduction

1. The Prime Minister of the People's Republic of Bangladesh, Her Excellency Begum Khaleda Zia, the King of Bhutan, His Majesty Jigme Singye Wangchuck, the Prime Minister of the Republic of India, His Excellency Mr. P.V. Narasimha Rao, the President of the Republic of Maldives, His Excellency Mr. Maumoon Abdul Gayoom, the Prime Minister of Nepal, the Rt. Hon. Manmohan Adhikari, the President of the Islamic Republic of Pakistan, His Excellency Mr. Farooq Ahmad Khan Leghari and the President of the Democratic Socialist Republic of Sri Lanka, Her Excellency Mrs. Chandrika Bandaranaike Kumaratunga met at the Eighth Summit of the South

Asian Association for Regional Cooperation (SAARC) at New Delhi, India on 2-4 May 1995.

SAARC Decade

2. The Heads of State or Government expressed their satisfaction on the achievements of the First Decade of SAARC and resolved to celebrate its completion of the First Decade both in the individual Member States and collectively. They endorsed the proposal of the Council of Ministers to convene a Commemorative Session of the Council on the theme "SAARC - Vision for the Second Decade" to identify the areas on which SAARC should focus in its Second Decade.

Regional Cooperation

3. The Heads of State or Government reaffirmed their resolve to intensify regional cooperation in order to accelerate the process of promoting the welfare and improving the quality of life of the peoples of South Asia. They reiterated their commitment to the principles and objectives enshrined in the SAARC Charter, particularly, to the principles of sovereign equality, territorial integrity, national independence, non-use of force and non-interference in each other's internal affairs. They recalled their conviction that in an increasingly interdependent world, regional cooperation was a dynamic instrument for promoting economic prosperity, mutual understanding and good neighbourly relations to achieve the objectives of peace and stability in South Asia. In this context, a climate of peace and stability would contribute to the economic growth.

Eradication of Poverty in South Asia

4. The Heads of State or Government reaffirmed their commitment to the eradication of poverty in South Asia, preferably by the year 2002 A.D. through an Agenda of Action.

5. The Leaders endorsed the recommendations of the Finance/Planning Ministers' Meeting held in Dhaka in July 1994 which recommended that a mechanism should be set up which would act as a forum for exchange of information on poverty eradication programmes, in the context of the policies and strategies adopted, particularly exchange of information on technologies that are relevant to efforts at poverty eradication. They agreed that this process could be strengthened by sharing and exchanging relevant studies carried out by independent research institutions and experts. This mechanism would be in the form of a three-tier institutional structure as recommended in the Report and would meet once a year. They noted that such a mechanism has been set up enabling the procedures of exchange of information to commence and welcomed the offer of India to host the first round of the three-tier mechanism.

6. The Heads of State or Government directed that the next meeting of Finance/Planning Ministers consider the efficacy of such mechanism towards eradicating poverty in the region and report on the progress achieved to the Ninth SAARC Summit, through the Council of Ministers.

7. In this context, they decided to declare 1995 as the "SAARC Year of Poverty Eradication".

8. Acknowledging that the abiding human qualities of dignity, creativity and productive potential are eroded by chronic poverty, the Heads of State or Government reiterated their commitment to empowering the poor for enhanced growth consistent with human development and equity.

9. Recognizing that poverty is a complex multi-dimensional problem with origins in both national and international domains, country-specific programmes to tackle poverty and international efforts supporting national efforts and the parallel process of creating a supportive international environment conducive to economic growth and social development of developing countries, are crucial for a solution to this problem. The World Summit for Social Development recognized the need for focusing the attention of the international community on and support the special needs of countries and regions in which there are substantial concentrations of people living in poverty, in particular those in South Asia and which face serious difficulties in achieving social and economic development. The Heads of State or Government reiterated their commitment to eradicate poverty and noted with appreciation the outcome of the World Summit for Social Development.

10. The Heads of State or Government committed themselves to addressing the fundamental causes of poverty and to provide for the basic needs of all. They reaffirmed their commitment to work for guaranteeing the realisation of the rights of all, in particular those of the poor, to food, work, shelter, health, education, resources and information.

11. The Heads of State or Government reaffirmed their commitment to provide expanded opportunities to the poor to enhance their overall capacities and improve living conditions and to adequate economic and social protection during unemployment, disability and old age. While recognising the need to improve, expand and deregulate markets to promote sustained economic growth they felt it was essential to mitigate any negative features created by the market forces and make all efforts to make the markets friendly to the poor. The Heads of State or Government reaffirmed the necessity to ensure that financial systems and other public policies are geared towards poverty eradication and warned against increase in socially divisive disparities.

12. The Heads of State or Government agreed that the Governments of SAARC countries will have to play a lead role in promoting the support structures needed for poverty eradication, including people's institutions and non-governmental organisations in the context of organising the people and fostering decentralisation and local self-governance and encouraging organisation of the poor, in the context of their social and economic interests.

SAARC Preferential Trading Arrangement (SAPTA)

13. The Heads of State or Government noted with satisfaction that subsequent to the signing of the Framework Agreement on SAARC Preferential Trading Arrangement (SAPTA) during their Seventh Summit in Dhaka in April 1993, the first round of trade negotiations to exchange trade concessions among Member States has been completed. They

directed that all necessary steps should be taken to facilitate ratification by all Member States and operationalise SAPTA by the end of 1995 as mandated.

14. The Leaders reiterated their firm belief that the operationalisation of SAPTA will herald the beginning of a new and significant process of regional cooperation and would lend strength to SAARC as an institution for promoting the welfare of the peoples of South Asia.

15. In view of the fast changing international economic environment, creation of major trading and economic groupings, establishment of the World Trade Organisation subsequent to the successful conclusion of the Uruguay Round of Multilateral Trade Negotiations and unilateral economic liberalisation measures being adopted by Member Countries, the Heads of State or Government emphasised the urgency of broadening and deepening cooperation within a specific and rapid time-frame in the core areas of trade and economic relations in the region. These developments call for added urgency to achieve more progress towards operationalisation of SAPTA and intensification of cooperation to expand regional trade. To that end, they decided that the "Components" and "Additional Measures" identified in Articles 4 and 6 respectively of the SAPTA Agreement should be implemented.

Integrated Programme of Action

16. The Heads of State or Government noted the progress made through the Integrated Programme of

Action covering a number of crucial areas and activities.

Regional Centres

17. The Leaders welcomed the establishment of the SAARC Documentation Centre (SDC) in New Delhi in May 1994 and the SAARC Meteorological Research Centre (SMRC) at Dhaka in January this year.

Women in Development

18. Noting that increased political and social consciousness in the region had highlighted the issues of elimination of gender-disparity and empowerment of women which are essential for their socio-economic development, the Heads of State or Government underlined the urgency of addressing these issues through further affirmative action.

19. The Leaders endorsed the "Kathmandu Resolution on Women and Family Health", adopted by the Ministerial Conference on Women and Family Health in Kathmandu in November 1993, and expressed satisfaction that appropriate programmes were being undertaken to implement the Resolution at the national level by the Member States.

20. The Leaders noted the progress in the implementation of the Plan of Action to mark 1991-2000 as the 'SAARC Decade of the Girl-Child', and requested the Council of Ministers to conduct a comprehensive mid-decade review for presentation to the Ninth SAARC Summit.

21. Recognising the serious threat faced by certain groups of Girl Children in Especially Difficult Circumstances (GCEDC) including those orphaned, disabled and exploited, the Leaders decided that an urgent appraisal of the situation of these children be undertaken by the Council of Ministers and specific recommendations be presented to the Ninth SAARC Summit.

22. Considering that the exploitation of the Girl Child is a direct reflection of the status of women in society, the Leaders reaffirmed their resolve to take necessary measures to eliminate all forms of discrimination against women and girl-children.

Children

23. The Heads of State or Government expressed satisfaction that the annual reviews of the situation of children in SAARC countries for the years 1993 and 1994 had been completed which indicated reduction in infant mortality and significant progress in the immunisation programme for children in the region.

24. Recalling the mid-decade goals of the World Summit for Children, the Heads of State or Government resolved to intensify their efforts both at the national and regional levels for attainment of these goals.

25. The Leaders welcomed that all Member States have become party to the Convention on the Rights of the Child. They felt that the recently held Cairo International Conference on Population and Development (ICPD) in September 1994 and the Copenhagen World Summit on Social Development in March 1995 had imparted fresh impetus to the on-

going efforts for the survival, protection and development of children in South Asia.

Youth

26. The Heads of State or Government endorsed the Malé Resolution on Youth adopted by the Ministerial Conference on Youth in South Asia held in the Maldives in May 1994 and noted that the Conference had, inter-alia, served to focus attention on the status of the youth and the challenges faced by them. The Leaders noted with satisfaction that the Agenda for Action incorporated in the Resolution is being implemented by Member States with a view to integrating the youth into the process of national development. They noted with satisfaction that the SAARC Youth Resolution had been adopted and the SAARC Youth Awards Scheme has been established.

27. The Leaders expressed satisfaction on the implementation of the Plan of Action to mark 1994 as the SAARC Year of the Youth in Member States and resolved to continue the momentum generated in Member States.

Persons With Disability

28. The Heads of State or Government noted with satisfaction that the Ministerial Conference on Disabled Persons was held in Islamabad in December 1993. They endorsed the Islamabad Resolution on Disabled Persons and the recommendations of the Conference and noted that the Conference had further increased awareness among the peoples of

South Asia regarding the needs and problems of the disabled persons. They welcomed the activities and programmes launched by the Member States in pursuance of the Resolution for the protection and promotion of persons with disability.

Shelter

29. The Heads of State or Government, recognising that housing was a basic right for all people and that, in addition to governmental efforts, private initiatives of the people and non-governmental agencies should be supported, reaffirmed their commitment to work towards the global objective of "Shelter for All by the Year 2000."

Literacy

30. The Heads of State or Government noted that illiteracy is one of the major causes of poverty, backwardness and social injustices and called on the Member States to initiate more concrete programmes aimed at eradicating illiteracy in the region preferably by the year 2000 A.D. They decided to observe 1996 as the "SAARC Year of Literacy".

Environment

31. Reaffirming the need for a concerted action for the protection and preservation of the environment, the Heads of State or Government expressed their satisfaction over the formulation of a common position by Member States prior to the World

Conference on Natural Disaster Reduction and the presentation of the collective position at the Yokohama Conference. They recognised that international cooperation is vital for building up national capabilities, transfer of appropriate technology and promotion of multilateral projects and research efforts in natural disaster reduction.

32. The Heads of State or Government expressed their deep concern at the unabated degradation of the environment and recurrence of devastating natural disasters. They also underscored the risks and dangers involved in overlooking the challenge posed by these problems. They expressed their commitment to implementing at all levels - national, bilateral, regional and global - programmes for the protection and preservation of the environment and prevention of its degradation. The Heads of State or Government stressed the importance of continuing the on-going SAARC activities in the field of environment.

33. The Heads of State or Government noted that although some work has been carried out in the area of disseminating information on the problems of environmental degradation and their impact on the region, progress in the implementation of the recommendations of the SAARC Regional Study on the Causes and Consequences of Natural Disasters and the Protection and Preservation of the Environment and the Regional Study on Greenhouse Effect and its Impact on the Region, which were completed in 1992, had been slow. They stressed the importance of effective and speedy implementation of the recommendations of the two Studies and requested Member States to take all necessary steps without further delay in vital areas such as sharing

and developing scientific capabilities to protect and manage the environment. They further directed the Technical Committee on Environment to monitor the progress made in the implementation of the recommendations of the two Studies, and submit a report to the Ninth Summit through the Council of Ministers.

34. The Heads of State or Government recalled the decisions expressed in the Dhaka Declaration of April, 1993 on the outcome of the United Nations Conference on Environment and Development (UNCED) of June, 1992 and reiterated the urgent need to ensure the flow of new and additional resources that are adequate and predictable to successfully implement the programmes of Agenda 21. They also recalled the United Nations minimum target for developed countries of 0.7 percent of GNP as Official Development Assistance, a target which is yet to be approximated by most developed countries. The Heads of State or Government also noted that international actions in the area of environment protection should be based on partnership and collective endeavours and should reflect the principle enunciated in the UNCED, of common but differentiated responsibilities. Integral to such actions is the promotion of economic growth in developing countries, that is both sustained and sustainable and direct action in eradicating poverty.

35. The Heads of State or Government also noted that the Commission on Sustainable Development set up to monitor the implementation of the Rio agreements has met thrice since their earlier meeting and expressed the hope that the Commission would be

able to facilitate the necessary flow of resources and technology.

36. The Heads of State or Government also noted that the Convention on Biological Diversity and the United Nations Framework Convention on Climate Change have both come into force and the first meetings of the Conferences of Parties to each Convention have been held. Welcoming these developments they urged that developing countries should be assisted in meeting their commitments under the Conventions. The establishment of the restructured Global Environment Facility (GEF) is a beginning in this direction. However, the Heads of State or Government urged that funds of a much larger order would be necessary if the needs of the Conventions are to be met.

Terrorism

37. The Heads of State or Government expressed serious concern on the spread of terrorism in and outside the region and reiterated their unequivocal condemnation of all acts, methods and practices of terrorism as criminal. They deplored all such acts for their ruinous impact on life, property, socio-economic development and political stability as well as on regional and international peace and cooperation.

38. The Heads of State or Government once again emphasised that highest priority should be accorded to the enactment of enabling legislation at the national level to give effect to the SAARC Regional Convention on Suppression of Terrorism. They urged Member States, which had not yet done so, to enact

expeditiously enabling legislation at the national level to implement the convention and reiterated the need for a constant dialogue and interaction among the concerned agencies of Member States, including submission of periodic recommendations to the Council of Ministers.

39. They underlined that cooperation among SAARC Member States was vital if the scourge of terrorism was to be eliminated from the region.

Drug Trafficking

40. The Heads of State or Government recognised that drug abuse and drug trafficking with its linkages with organised crime, illicit arms trade and terrorism continues to pose a serious threat to the security and stability in the region.

41. While noting the efforts made by Member States as well as the regional cooperation underway to combat this pernicious trade, the Leaders stressed the urgency of further strengthening the process of cooperation.

42. The Leaders welcomed the ratification of the SAARC Convention on Narcotic Drugs and Psychotropic Substances by all Member States and entry into force of the Convention in September 1993. They urged all Member States to take necessary follow-up action for effective implementation of the Convention.

Science and Technology

43. The Heads of State or Government reiterated that cooperation in the area of Science and Technology

should be accorded high priority. Noting that some progress had been made towards establishment of networking arrangements, inter-alia, in the fields of Bio-Technology, Genetic Engineering, Energy Modelling Techniques and Low-Cost Housing and Building Technologies, the Leaders called for further acceleration of this process.

People-to-People Contact

44. Reiterating their earlier resolve to further promote people-to-people contact through increased involvement of the peoples of South Asia in the process of regional cooperation, the Heads of State or Government noted with satisfaction that such interaction has been taking place through various fora both within and outside the SAARC framework and has contributed to the promotion of mutual understanding in the region.

45. The Leaders noted that SAARCLAW (an association for persons of the legal communities of SAARC countries) had been accorded recognition by SAARC. The Leaders hoped that SAARCLAW would play an effective role in fostering closer cooperation among the legal communities in the region.

46. The Leaders noted with satisfaction that the SAARC Chamber of Commerce and Industry (SCCI) has been functioning satisfactorily. They expressed hope that the SAARC Chamber and its constituent units in the Member States will do their utmost to promote trade and economic cooperation in the SAARC region. The Leaders commended the SAARC Chamber for disseminating information on the scope, content and

potentials of SAARC Preferential Trading Arrangement (SAPTA) among the business community in the region.

47. The Heads of State or Government expressed satisfaction that the SAARC Visa Exemption Scheme is being implemented smoothly and has enhanced the scope of people-to-people contacts.

South Asian Development Fund (SADF)

48. The Heads of State or Government endorsed the establishment of a three-window South Asian Development Fund with the merger of SAARC Fund for Regional Projects and the SAARC Regional Fund and a third window for social development and infrastructure development.

Projection of Collective Positions

49. The Heads of State or Government recalled their decision taken at the Seventh SAARC Summit regarding development of collective positions in international fora on such issues as would enhance the international profile of South Asia and would enable the Member States to articulate their position on them more effectively. They noted that Council of Ministers had formulated a procedure for projection of SAARC collective positions at such international fora.

50. They noted with satisfaction that pursuant to the decision at the Seventh SAARC Summit, collective positions were formulated by Member States which were presented at the World Conference on Natural

Disaster Reduction and the World Summit for Social Development. The Leaders also noted with satisfaction that a SAARC collective position will also be presented at the Fourth World Conference on Women in Beijing in September 1995.

Security of Small States

51. The Heads of State or Government reaffirming their commitment to universally accepted principles and norms relating to the sovereign rights and territorial integrity of all States, recognised that small States, because of their particular problems, required special measures of support for safeguarding their independence and territorial integrity. They reiterated that real protection of small and weaker States should be firmly rooted in the rule of law. This, they stressed should be ensured by all countries either severally or collectively through the pursuit of appropriate actions.

International Political Departments

52. The Heads of State or Government noted that the end of the Cold War had resulted in fundamental changes in the political landscape. It was therefore important that a new idiom be found to address new concerns. The disappearance of the confrontation between the two power blocs presented an opportunity towards building a genuine consensus for a new international order.

53. The Heads of State or Government had wide ranging discussions on the current global political trends and

future prospects, particularly those issues that concern South Asia. In this context, they reiterated their deep commitment to the purposes and principles of the UN Charter and reaffirmed their resolve to strengthen the United Nations as the central instrument for peace, security, disarmament, development and cooperation among the nations of the world. While pledging their support to all constructive initiatives aimed at strengthening the United Nations, the Leaders emphasised that such initiatives must be undertaken with the sole objective of rendering the United Nations and all its organs more democratic, efficient and effective and not to limit the focus of its attention to a narrow and isolated range of objectives.

54. Appreciating the role of some SAARC Member States in the UN Peace Keeping Operations in various parts of the world, the Heads of State or Government felt that such participation had contributed towards maintenance of peace and security in the world.

55. The Heads of State or Government reiterated their firm commitment to the principles and objectives of the Non-aligned Movement and underlined the continued validity and relevance of these principles and objectives in the contemporary world. They recalled the stabilising role played by the Movement in global affairs since its inception. They expressed their deep conviction that the Movement's innate strength equipped it to continue to play a most constructive role in laying the foundations of a new world order based on the rule of law, non-discrimination, equity and cooperation.

56. The Heads of State or Government noted that while the international community had successfully created the norm against chemical and biological weapons, it had, unfortunately, been unable to do the same with regard to nuclear weapons. The Leaders were convinced that more needs to be done and at a far greater pace. Reiterating that the utmost priority was to be given to nuclear disarmament, given the danger posed by nuclear weapons, they urged the Conference on Disarmament to negotiate an international convention prohibiting the use or threat of use of nuclear weapons under any circumstances and undertake negotiations for the complete elimination of all nuclear weapons within a time bound framework.

57. The Heads of State or Government expressed their strong commitment to the promotion and protection of human rights. They agreed to take all necessary steps to achieve this objective.

International Economic and Social Issues

58. The Heads of State or Government welcomed the successful conclusion of the Uruguay Round of multilateral trade negotiations and reaffirmed their commitment to implement fully and as scheduled, the Final Act of the Uruguay Round of multilateral trade negotiations. They also welcomed the coming into existence of the WTO and expressed the hope that it would help to expand international trade, particularly that of the developing countries. They reaffirmed the immediate need to elaborate policies to enable developing countries, to take advantage of

expanded international trading opportunities, in the context of the full implementation of the Round. They called on all countries to refrain from any unilateral measure not in accordance with international law, the Charter of the United Nations and enlightened regionalism and globalism that creates obstacles to trade relations among States and thereby impedes the full realisation of social and economic development.

59. Recognising that the promotion of mutually reinforcing broad-based sustained economic growth on a global scale, as well as a non-discriminatory, and multilateral rule-based international trading system, provided a basis for social development, the Heads of State or Government called for the establishment of an open, equitable, cooperative and mutually beneficial international economic environment. They also called for a reduction of trade barriers and promotion of expanded access to global markets.

60. The Heads of State or Government reaffirmed their commitment to safeguard the basic interests of workers. They called upon countries to refrain from erecting trade barriers in the guise of promotion and protection of workers' rights. They deplored the tendency to impose any conditionalities on international trade, whether as a "social clause" or as the "environmental clause", while reiterating their commitment to ensuring workers' rights as well as protection of the environment.

Special Measures for the Least Developed and Land-Locked Countries

61. The Heads of State or Government noted with deep concern that economic growth in the Least Developed Countries and Land-Locked Countries is not satisfactory and emphasised the need to take special measures for accelerating the process of development. They reiterated the need to fulfil the internationally agreed aid targets for the developing countries and the Least Developed Countries. They emphasised on the need for exceptional finance to facilitate implementation of economic reform programmes in SAARC Countries.

Dates and Venue of the Ninth Meeting of the SAARC heads of State or Government

62. The Heads of State or Government gratefully accepted the offer of the Government of Maldives to host the Ninth SAARC Summit. The dates would be finalised in consultation with Member States.

63. The Heads of State or Government of Bangladesh, Bhutan, Maldives, Nepal, Pakistan and Sri Lanka expressed their deep appreciation for the exemplary manner in which the Prime Minister of India had discharged his responsibilities as Chairman of the Meeting. They expressed their profound gratitude for the warm and gracious hospitality extended to them by the Government and the people of the Republic of India and for the excellent arrangements made for the Meeting.

12

Declaration of the Ninth SAARC Summit, Male'

The Male' Declaration of the Heads of State or Government of the Member Countries of South Asian Association for Regional Cooperation issued on 14th May 1997.

Introduction

1. The Prime Minister of the People's Republic of Bangladesh, Her Excellency Sheikh Hasina; the King of Bhutan, His Majesty Jigme Singye Wangchuck; the Prime Minister of the Republic of India, His Excellency Mr. Inder Kumar Gujral; the President of the Republic of Maldives, His Excellency Mr. Maumoon Abdul Gayoom; the Prime Minister of Kingdom of Nepal, Rt. Hon. Mr. Lokendra Bahadur Chand; the Prime Minister of the Islamic Republic of Pakistan, His Excellency Mr. Mohammad Nawaz Sharif and the President of the Democratic Socialist Republic of Sri Lanka, Her Excellency Mrs. Chandrika Bandaranaike Kumaratunga met at the

Ninth Summit of the South Asian Association for Regional Co-operation (SAARC) at Malé, Maldives on 12-14 May 1997.

Regoinal Cooperation

2. The Heads of State or Government reiterated their commitment to SAARC and resolved to accelerate regional cooperation in order to realise the aims and objectives of the Association. They reaffirmed their commitment to the principles enshrined in the SAARC Charter, especially to the principles of sovereign equality, territorial integrity, national independence, non-use of force and non-interference in each others' internal affairs. They were convinced that regional cooperation was indispensable in an interdependent world for the realisation of the full potential of the South Asian region.

3. The Heads of State or Government welcomed the holding of the Commemorative Session of the Council of Ministers in New Delhi in December 1995 to mark the First Decade, on the theme "SAARC - Vision for the Second Decade". They observed that over the past decade SAARC has matured as an institution and the scope and volume of cooperative activities have expanded. They expressed satisfaction that in addition to continued cooperation in agreed areas, SAARC has now moved into the core areas of economic cooperation.

4. The Heads of State or Government noted that, in the twelve years of its existence, SAARC has seen progress in various fields of its endeavour. They directed that a Group of Eminent Persons (GEP) be

constituted, with distinguished backgrounds in activities pertaining to regional cooperation, comprising of one representative from each Member State, with the discretion of each Member State to appoint an additional representative. This Group, to which the SAARC Secretary-General will be invited, will undertake a comprehensive appraisal of SAARC, and identify measures including mechanisms to further vitalise and enhance the effectiveness of the Association in achieving its objectives. They further decided that the Group may develop a long-range vision and formulate a perspective plan of action including a SAARC Agenda for 2000 and Beyond which will spell out the target that can and must be achieved by the year 2020. The Group may report to the Heads of State or Government at the Tenth SAARC Summit.

5. With a view to enhancing the effectiveness of the role and functioning of the Secretariat, the Heads of State or Government agreed to amend Article V (1) of the Memorandum of Understanding on the Establishment of the Secretariat and decided that the tenure of the Secretary-General, with immediate effect, shall be for a non-renewable term of three years.

6. The Heads of State or Government reiterated their determination to reinforce the unity and cohesion of SAARC. With the objective of enhancing regional solidarity and promoting overall development within SAARC, the Heads of State or Government encouraged, under the provisions of Articles VII and X of the Charter, the development of specific projects relevant to the special individual needs of three or more Member States.

7. They agreed that a climate of mutual accommodation and purposeful cooperation was needed to impart further impetus to the SAARC process during the second decade of SAARC in order to address the developmental challenges facing the region.

Enhancing Political Cooperation

8. The Heads of State or Government recalled their commitment to the promotion of mutual trust and understanding and, recognising that the aims of promoting peace, stability and amity and accelerated socio-economic cooperation may best be achieved by fostering good neighbourly relations, relieving tensions and building confidence, agreed that a process of informal political consultations would prove useful in this regard.

Eradication of Poverty in South Asia

9. The Heads of State or Government were unequivocal in their commitment to the eradication of poverty in South Asia at the earliest, preferably by the year 2002 A.D. through an Agenda of Action. They noted with satisfaction the establishment of a three-tier mechanism on poverty eradication and endorsed the recommendations of the two rounds of meetings under this mechanism hosted by India and Pakistan, respectively. They desired that the Ministers of Finance / Planning should meet again in the near future to give further impetus to this process.

10. In considering the Report of the Ministers of Finance/Planning, the Heads of State or Government

agreed that effective implementation of poverty eradication programmes required a focus on greater participation of target groups in the formulation and implementation of such programmes through social mobilization. They, therefore, decided to designate 1997 as the "SAARC Year of Participatory Governance".

11. The Heads of State or Government welcomed the successful holding of the Micro-credit Summit in Washington, D.C. in February 1997 and its Declaration of support to launch a global campaign to reach 100 million of the world's poorest families, especially women, with credit for self-employment and other financial and business services, by the year 2005 A.D.

12. Recognising that micro-credit programmes have successfully demonstrated their usefulness toward achieving many goals of socio-economic upliftment, including the eradication of poverty and empowerment of women, the Leaders agreed to intensify endeavours in their respective countries so that the outreach of these programmes becomes widespread.

13. The Heads of State or Government were convinced that an enabling international environment to support poverty eradication efforts of the SAARC countries is an essential element in attaining success for these efforts. They urged all donor countries, international institutions and other bodies engaged in eradication of poverty to increase their support and assistance to these efforts.

Acceleration of Economic Cooperation

14. The Heads of State or Government noted with satisfaction the entry into force of the Agreement on SAARC Preferential Trading Arrangement (SAPTA) on 7 December 1995. They recognised the importance of achieving a free trade area by the year 2001 A.D. and reiterated that steps towards trade liberalisation must take into account the special needs of the smaller and the Least Developed Countries and that benefits must accrue equitably.

15. While expressing satisfaction at the conclusion of the two Rounds of Trade Negotiations under SAPTA, the Heads of State or Government welcomed the decision to launch the Third Round of Trade Negotiations shortly. They agreed that preferential tariff concessions should cover products which are being actively traded amongst Member States. They further agreed that the Third Round should deepen tariff concessions along with the removal of non-tariff barriers and structural impediments in order to move speedily towards the goal of SAFTA.

16. The Leaders welcomed the holding of the First Meeting of the Commerce Ministers and the First SAARC Trade Fair in New Delhi in 1996 and noted the decision of the Commerce Ministers to meet annually. They further welcomed the offer of Pakistan to host the second SAARC Trade Fair to coincide with the SAARC Commerce Ministers' Meeting.

17. The Heads of State or Government agreed that the efforts to enhance trade and economic co-operation in the region would be further strengthened by

initiating specific steps to promote and protect investment, increase complementarities in economic activities of Member States and other measures supportive of promotion of SAARC joint ventures. They also welcomed the offer of India to host a meeting on promotion and protection of investment and the offer of Pakistan to host a meeting on avoidance of double taxation. They also welcomed measures of cooperation in the areas of customs standardisation, arbitration and enhancing industrial economy and management.

18. The Heads of State or Government agreed that in intensifying economic cooperation the interests of smaller countries, especially the least developed among them, should be taken into account through the implementation of special measures in their favour.

19. The Heads of State or Government noted that inadequate communications facilities amongst the Member States were a major hindrance to closer economic co-operation. They stressed the importance of developing infrastructure and adequate communication networks among Member States to reinforce the process of economic co-operation. In this regard, they highlighted the need for the simplification of complex documentation procedures and transactional software to facilitate economic interaction across the region. They welcomed the offer of Sri Lanka to host a Meeting of the Communication Ministers of the Member States.

20. The Heads of State or Government reaffirmed their determination to encourage the private sector in the region to contribute increasingly to the strengthening

of intra-SAARC links in key areas of trade, investment and finance. They welcomed the decision by the SCCI to convene annually an Economic Cooperation Conference in conjunction with the annual meeting of SAARC Commerce Ministers and SAARC Trade Fairs.

Integrated Programme of Action (IPA)

21. The Heads of State or Government emphasised the need to make the Integrated Programme of Action (IPA) more effective through the selection of target-oriented and time-bound activities within an overall framework of enhanced co-operation among Member States. In this context, they noted that the Secretary-General had been authorised by the Council of Ministers to constitute a Group of Experts to review the IPA.

Reginal Centres

22. The Heads of State or Government noted that Regional Centres have an important role to play in harnessing the resources and capabilities within the SAARC region in addressing specific and shared concerns of Member States. They welcomed the decision of the Council of Ministers to establish a Human Resource Development Centre in Pakistan.

23. They stressed that Regional Centres should implement action and result- oriented programmes and highlighted the importance of rationalising the functioning of these Centres.

Women in Development

24. The Heads of State or Government recognised that increased social and political awareness in the region had brought positive contributions to the issues of gender equality and empowerment of women. They further emphasized the need for enhanced cooperation to achieve the desired objective of bringing women into the mainstream of socio-economic development in the region. In this context, they emphasised the urgency to effectively implement the recommendations of the "Dhaka Resolution on Women", issued at the conclusion of the SAARC Ministerial Conference on Women and presented to the Fourth World Conference on Women.

25. Taking note of the mid-decade review of the SAARC Plan of Action on the Girl-Child, the Heads of State or Government expressed their determination to accelerate efforts at reduction of malnutrition and mortality rates, raising education and literacy rates, reduction of the proportion of early marriage among girls, and the postponement of the age of first pregnancy, thereby contributing to the increased welfare of the girl-child and reduction of population growth rates.

26. The Heads of State or Government reaffirmed their commitment to take urgent action to alleviate the situation of Girl Children in Especially Difficult Circumstances (GCEDC), including those orphaned, disabled and/or exploited. In this context, they endorsed the recommendations made by the Council of Ministers, aimed at the creation of a socio-economic environment in the SAARC region which

would provide equal opportunities to children from all economic sections.

27. Expressing grave concern at the trafficking of women and children within and between countries, the Heads of State or Government pledged to coordinate their efforts and take effective measures to address this problem. They decided that existing legislation in Member States should be strengthened and strictly enforced. This should include simplification of repatriation procedures for victims of trafficking. They also decided that the feasibility of establishing a Regional Convention on Combating the Crime of Trafficking in Women and Children for Prostitution be examined by the relevant Technical Committee.

Children

28. The Heads of State or Government expressed satisfaction that the annual reviews of the situation of children in SAARC countries for the years 1995 and 1996 revealed significant progress in reducing infant mortality and in enhancing the coverage of immunisation in the region. They stressed that sustained efforts should be made by Member States to consolidate the gains in these areas. In this regard, they welcomed the decision to designate Seventh December, 1997 and Eighteenth January, 1998 as "SAARC Polio Immunisation Days".

29. The Heads of State or Government resolved to implement appropriate policies at the national level to achieve the targets and objectives set out in the Rawalpindi Declaration issued at the end of the Third Ministerial Conference on the Children of South Asia

held in August 1996, including the call to eliminate the evil of child-labour from the region by the year 2010 A.D. They called for stringent measures to protect children from all forms of exploitation. To this end, the Leaders agreed to set up a Study Group at an appropriate level to examine the social compulsions that create the problem.

30. They reaffirmed their commitment to improve the status of children in disadvantaged circumstances in the SAARC region. They recognised that the problems of these children are inextricably linked to the prevailing socio-economic conditions and problems of the region, and therefore, called for a holistic approach to address them. They expressed the need to formulate a Convention on Regional Arrangements on the Promotion of Child Welfare in South Asia in launching the SAARC Decade of the Rights of the Child, from the year 2001 A.D. to 2010 A.D.

Nutrition

31. Noting that malnutrition, often severe, is a serious concern in South Asia, the Heads of State or Government agreed to launch an Initiative on Nutrition aimed at promotion of availability of food of essential nutritional value to individual household and evolving policies for supplementing and fortifying essential micro-nutrients, deficiencies of which have affected the well being of the most vulnerable sections of the population, particularly women and children.

32. The Heads of State or Government emphasised that the provision of a safe, secure and clean environment was an essential pre-requisite for the welfare of the most vulnerable sections of society in the region, particularly for the proper growth and development of children, and agreed on the need for launching technology missions to develop low-cost, easily replicable technologies appropriate local conditions for sustainable harvesting of water, provision of clean drinking water and sanitation.

Youth

33. The Heads of State or Government welcomed the operationalization of the SAARC Youth Awards Scheme and noted that the Scheme will be reviewed in the near future with the purpose of expanding it. They also welcomed the initiative to organize Youth Camps in the region on various themes.

Persons with Disability

34. Conscious of the continuing problems faced by disabled persons, the Heads of State or Government reaffirmed their resolve to continue the implementation of the recommendations of the Ministerial Conference on Disabled Persons held in Islamabad in December 1993.

Shelter

35. The Heads of State or Government emphasized that housing was a basic right of all people and reiterated

their determination to sustain efforts to improve the condition of human settlements in the region, with a view to achieving the global objective of "Shelter for All by the Year 2000".

Literacy

36. The Heads of State or Government recognised that illiteracy is one of the major causes impeding the development of the vast human resource potential of the region and a major factor contributing to the region's economic backwardness and social imbalance. They noted that the Member States had observed "1996 as the SAARC Year of Literacy" and reiterated their commitment to continue endeavours to eradicate illiteracy from the region.

37. Recognising the resource, manpower and infrastructural constraints to the promotion of vocational and higher education in the region, the Leaders agreed that new and innovative methods like Open Learning and Distance Education can play an effective role in meeting regional needs in a cost effective and flexible manner. Accordingly, they agreed that the institutional facilities in such education available in the region should be utilised on a regional scale. The possibility of the creation of a Consortium of Open Universities in the region should also be explored.

Environment

38. The Heads of State or Government expressed concern about the continuing degradation of the environment

in different parts of the world including the SAARC region. While recognizing that collective initiatives were required urgently to address the challenge posed by such degradation, they noted that unsustainable consumption patterns in the developed countries and widespread poverty in the developing countries are major factors contributing to ecological degradation in different parts of the world. In this regard, they noted that although both developed and developing countries were required to undertake specific initiatives to face environmental concerns, stress should also be laid on the acceleration of development in developing countries to enable them to face environmental challenges.

39. Reviewing the work carried out in the area of disseminating information on the problems of environmental degradation and their impact on the region, the Heads of State or Government expressed the urgent need for the implementation of the recommendations of the SAARC Regional Study on the Greenhouse Effect and its Impact on the Region, and the Regional Study on the Causes and Consequences of Natural Disasters and the Protection and Preservation of the Environment. They welcomed the offer of the Maldives to host a meeting of the SAARC Environment Ministers to focus more directly on the Environment concerns of the region including the formulation of a Plan of Action for immediate implementation of recommendations contained in the two Studies, taking into account the recommendations made by the Meeting of the Environment Ministers in New Delhi in April 1997. The Leaders felt that the meeting may also consider the feasibility of drawing up a Regional Treaty on

Environment in the context of existing international Conventions on the subject. They reiterated their view that Member States should take all necessary steps in vital areas such as sharing and developing scientific capabilities to protect and manage the environment.

40. The Heads of State or Government agreed on the urgent need for cooperation through exchange of information, strategies and technologies for combating pollution of air and water and for evolving common minimum standards which could be applied region-wide in this regard. Recognising the wealth of bio-diversity in the South Asian region and expressing concern at the threat of its progressive depletion through degradation and fragmentation, they affirmed their commitment to take steps towards the protection and conservation of these genetic resources. They noted that many areas rich in bio-diversity in South Asia lay along shared borders and agreed to cooperate in the creation of contiguous protected areas where identified. They also agreed to cooperate in the prevention of illegal trafficking in flora and fauna and devise an appropriate mechanism for this purpose, including the possibility of concluding a Convention. They decided that the meeting of SAARC Environment Ministers should be institutionalised henceforth as an annual event.

41. While expressing concern at the slow progress in the implementation of the Agenda 21, the Heads of State or Government called for the urgent implementation of the commitments, recommendations and agreements reached at the United Nations

Conference on Environment and Development held in Rio de Janeiro in June 1992. In particular, they also called for the early implementation of the United Nations Framework Convention on Climate Change and the adoption of a Protocol or another legal instrument for reduction of greenhouse gas emissions by developed countries within an early timeframe, but not later than the year 2005 A.D.

42. The Heads of State or Government underlined the importance of projecting an effective, and coordinated collective position of SAARC at the forthcoming Special Session of the United Nations General Assembly to Review and Appraise the Implementation of Agenda 21. In this regard, they fully endorsed the New Delhi Declaration issued at the end of the SAARC Ministerial Conference on Environment held from 2-3 April 1997, as amended at the Eighteenth Session of the Council of Ministers.

Terrorism and Drug Trafflicking

43. Recognising that terrorism and drug trafficking pose a serious threat to security and stability of Member States, the Heads of State or Government reiterated their firm commitment to combat these activities in the region. They emphasised the urgent need to complete enabling legislation in order to implement the SAARC Regional Conventions on Suppression of Terrorism and on Narcotic Drugs and Psychotropic Substances.

44. The Heads of State or Government recalled the adoption of the 1996 UN Declaration on Measures to Eliminate International Terrorism and urged all

Member States to work towards its implementation. They called for international action to prevent the abuse of Refugee Conventions and to halt activities which help terrorist groups to collect funds for their activities in South Asia.

45. The Heads of State or Government noted the establishment of the SAARC Terrorist Offences Monitoring Desk (STOMD) and the SAARC Drug Offences Monitoring Desk (SDOMD) in Colombo. They agreed on the need to maintain regular flow of relevant information to enable the Monitoring Desks to function effectively.

46. The Heads of State or Government noted with appreciation the convening of the First SAARC Conference on Cooperation in Police Matters in Colombo during July 1996. They endorsed the outcome of the Conference, particularly, the call for sharing of expertise with regard to the different areas of police investigation and investigation of organised crime and drug related crimes. They welcomed the offer of the Maldives to host the second Conference in 1997.

Science and Technology

47. Noting that cooperation in the field of Science and Technology was imperative in ensuring the acceleration of the process of development in the region and recognising the progress made in this field, the Heads of State or Government emphasised the need to continue cooperation in this area, especially in facilitating research and exchange of information in the fields of bio-technology, genetic

engineering, energy modelling techniques and low-cost housing and building technologies.

Tourism

48. Emphasising that tourism plays an important role in promoting people to people contact in the region, the Heads of State or Government stressed the importance of strengthening cooperation with the aim of realising its full potential in the region. They were convinced that greater cooperation in this area would contribute to the enhancement of people-to-people contact within the region as well as to the economic development of Member States.

49. The Heads of State or Government noted that organised tourism in South Asia has not yet achieved its full potential, and recommended that appropriate measures to promote tourism be given priority, and in this regard, welcomed the offer of Sri Lanka to host the SAARC Ministerial Meeting on Tourism in Colombo in 1997.

People-to-People Contact

50. The Heads of State or Government reiterated their conviction that enhanced people-to-people contact would contribute to strengthening mutual understanding and goodwill among the people in the region. In this context, they noted the positive contribution made by SAARC Chamber of Commerce and Industry (SCCI) and SAARCLAW.

51. They observed that SAARC Chairs, Fellowships and Scholarships Scheme should be increasingly used to

facilitate greater interaction among students, scholars and academics in the region.

52. The Heads of State or Government noted with satisfaction the inclusion of new categories of persons from different walks of life in the SAARC Visa Exemption Scheme and believed that this would further promote people-to-people contact.

53. They noted the offer of Sri Lanka to host the First SAARC Film Festival in Colombo in 1998 to coincide with the 50th anniversary of the Independence of Sri Lanka.

54. The Heads of State or Government agreed that the SAARC countries possess enormous tourism potential that should be properly utilised for the benefit of the people of the region. In this context, they decided that the civil aviation authorities of Member States should meet in the very near future with a view to establishing direct air services between SAARC capitals which would promote people-to-people contact and encourage tourism. They welcomed the offer of Bangladesh to host the first meeting of the civil aviation authorities.

South Asian Development Fund (SADF)

55. While expressing satisfaction that the South Asian Development Fund (SADF) had been established in June 1996 initially with its headquarters in Dhaka, Bangladesh, the Heads of State or Government recognised the need to make the Fund operational at the earliest.

Projection of Collective Positions

56. The Heads of State or Government reiterated their commitment to develop collective SAARC positions in international fora on issues of common concern, in order to enhance the international profile of South Asia as well as to enable Member States to articulate their position on such issues in a more effective manner. In this regard, they noted with satisfaction the collective SAARC positions finalised and presented prior to the Fourth World Conference on Women held in Beijing in September 1995, HABITAT II held in Istanbul in June 1996, and World Food Summit held in Rome in November 1996. They also expressed satisfaction with the formulation of a SAARC common position before the forthcoming Special Session of the United Nations General Assembly to Review and Appraise the Implementation of Agenda 21.

Security of Small State

57. The Heads of State or Government recognised that small states, because of their particular vulnerabilities, require special measures of support from the international community for safeguarding their sovereign independence and territorial integrity. They further reaffirmed their view that such support should be firmly rooted in the scrupulous adherence to the UN Charter, the rule of law and strict adherence to universally accepted principles and norms related to sovereign rights and territorial integrity of all States irrespective of size. This, they emphasised, may be ensured by all countries either

severally or collectively through the pursuit of appropriate action.

International Political Developments

58. The Heads of State or Government had wide ranging discussions on current international issues, particularly those that affect South Asia. In this context, reiterating their deep commitment to the purposes and principles of the UN Charter, the Heads of State or Government recalled that the commemoration of the 50th anniversary of the founding of the United Nations in October 1995 had highlighted the need to strengthen, revitalize and reform the Organization. They reiterated their support to the on-going process of restructuring and revitalizing the Organization and reaffirmed their resolve to make it a more effective universal instrument for addressing international issues on an equitable and democratic basis, taking full account of the interests and concerns of all states.

59. Addressing the question of reform of the United Nations, the Heads of State or Government laid particular emphasis on the principle of sovereign equality of States and on equitable geographical representation in regard to the question of increase in the membership of the Security Council. They recognised the need to make the Security Council more representative, democratic and transparent, so that it is better equipped to uphold its responsibility for the maintenance of international peace and security.

60. The Heads of State or Government reiterated their firm commitment to the principles and objectives of the Non-Aligned Movement (NAM) and underscored the continued validity and relevance of these principles and objectives in the contemporary world. They expressed their deep conviction that the Movement's innate strength equips it to continue to play a most constructive role in laying the foundations of a new world order based on the rule of law, non-interference, equity and cooperation.

61. The Heads of State or Government while expressing support to the continuation of the peace process in the Middle East, expressed concern at the setback to the peace process and unleashing of violence against Palestinian people in occupied territories and the resulting threat to the peace process due to policies of the Government of Israel in establishing and enlarging existing Jewish settlements in the occupied Palestinian territories. They were convinced that the peace process should be continued by honouring previous commitments made by all parties involved. They also called for the restoration of the inalienable rights of the Palestinian people, including the right of self determination and the establishment of a sovereign State under the leadership of PLO, their sole legitimate representative, which could co-exist with its neighbours in peace and harmony.

62. Noting that the end of the Cold War had created unprecedented opportunities in the field of disarmament, the Heads of State or Government recognised the need for the international community to pursue nuclear disarmament as a matter of highest priority. In this regard, they recognised the need to start negotiations through the Conference on

Disarmament and to establish a phased programme for the complete elimination of nuclear weapons within a specified framework of time, including a Nuclear Weapons Convention.

63. While reiterating their commitment to the promotion and protection of human rights, the Heads of State or Government resolved to take all necessary steps to achieve this objective.

International Economic and Social Issues

64. The Heads of State or Government noted that current trends of globalisation and liberalisation were imposing a heavy burden on developing economies, in particular, the least developed countries (LDCs) which are becoming marginalised from the mainstream of the world economy. They also expressed concern over trends to erect new protectionist barriers by linking imports from developing countries to politically motivated social and environmental values and concerns, such as human rights. They observed that the impact of these trends is compounded by new challenges relating to issues of access to markets, capital and new technologies. They also noted with regret the overall decline in the Official Development Assistance (ODA) over the years which has contributed to the aggravation of the condition of the LDCs.

65. The Heads of State or Government reaffirmed the promotion of a non-discriminatory and multilateral rule-based global system of economic relations in order to engage the developing countries constructively and on the basis of reciprocal shared

benefits in the process of liberalisation, as well as to assist them integrate into the global economy.

66. The Heads of State or Government called on the developed countries to assist the developing countries through the creation of a favourable and supportive global economic environment, in particular, through domestic action in their countries for purposes of accelerating investment flows to developing countries thereby generating a positive impact on the developmental efforts of developing countries as well as assisting their integration into the multilateral trading system. They also called on the developed countries to substantially reduce tariff and non-tariff barriers and desist from restrictive trade practices, which would negatively affect the access of developing countries to global markets.

Special Measures for the Least Developed and Land-Locked Countires

67. The Heads of State or Government emphasised the need for priority action on various international development commitments, such as the Paris Declaration and the Programme of Action for LDCs for the 1990s.

68. While noting with deep concern that economic growth in the Least Developed and Land-Locked Countries is not progressing well, the Heads of State or Government stressed the need to take special measures for accelerating the process of development. They emphasized the need to fulfil the internationally agreed aid targets for ensuring accelerated and sustained economic growth in

developing countries particularly in the Least Developed Countries. They stressed on the need for adequate resources to facilitate implementation of economic reform programmes in SAARC countries.

69. The Heads of State or Government emphasised that the review of the criteria for the determination of LDC status for consideration by the United Nations General Assembly this year, must take into account the special significance of the extent and magnitude of incidence of poverty in the poorest countries and the special vulnerabilities of small island states.

Dates and Venue of the Tenth Meeting of the Heads of the State Governments

70. The Heads of State or Government accepted with deep appreciation the offer of the Government of Sri Lanka to host the Tenth SAARC Summit. They further decided that the Eleventh and Twelfth Summits will be held in Nepal and Pakistan, respectively.

71. The Heads of State or Government of Bangladesh, Bhutan, India, Nepal, Pakistan and Sri Lanka expressed their sincere appreciation for the exemplary manner in which the President of the Republic of the Maldives had conducted the Meeting and guided its proceedings in his capacity as Chairman. They expressed their deep gratitude for the warm and generous hospitality extended to them by the Government and the people of the Maldives and for the excellent arrangements made for the Meeting.

13

Declaration of the Tenth SAARC Summit, Colombo

The Declaration of the Tenth SAARC Summit of the Heads of State or Government of the Member Countries of the South Asian Association for Regional Cooperation issued on 31 July 1998, in Colombo.

Introduction

1. The Prime Minister of the People's Republic of Bangladesh, Her Excellency Sheikh Hasina; Chairman, Council of Ministers and Head of Government of the Royal Government of Bhutan, His Excellency Lyonpo Jigmi Y. Thinley; the Prime Minister of the Republic of India, His Excellency Mr. Atal Behari Vajpayee; the President of the Republic of Maldives, His Excellency Mr. Maumoon Abdul Gayoom; the Prime Minister of the Kingdom of Nepal, Rt. Hon. Mr. Girija Prasad Koirala; the Prime Minister of the Islamic Republic of Pakistan, His Excellency Mr. Muhammad Nawaz Sharif; and the

President of the Democratic Socialist Republic of Sri Lanka, Her Excellency Mrs. Chandrika Bandaranaike Kumaratunga met at the Tenth Summit of the South Asian Association for Regional Cooperation (SAARC) at Colombo from July 29 to 31, 1998, in the year of the Golden Jubilee of the Independence of Sri Lanka.

Regional Cooperation

2. The Heads of State or Government re-affirmed their firm commitment to the objectives, principles and provisions of the Charter of the South Asian Association for Regional Cooperation (SAARC) and to the pursuit of regional cooperation on the basis of their acceptance of the principles of sovereign equality, territorial integrity of States, political independence, non-interference in each others internal affairs, non-use of force, the peaceful settlement of all disputes and mutuality of benefit.
3. The Heads of State or Government recognised that the rich potential for productive, equitable regional cooperation among the Governments and people of South Asia which accounts for a fifth of humanity should be fully realised.

Cultural Unity

4. The Heads of State or Government recognized that South Asia, while reflecting a rich, complex and varied plurality of cultural and religious traditions, was heir to a profound common civilizational continuum of great antiquity which constitutes a historical basis for sustaining harmonious relations

among the people of the region. They acknowledged that the SAARC process could draw more deeply from the vitality and strength of South Asia's shared cultural heritage as a source influencing and enhancing creative energies in all fields.

5. The Heads of State or Government welcomed the offer of Sri Lanka to host a meeting of the Ministers of Cultural Affairs of SAARC to prepare a practical Action Plan to network the national institutes of cultural relations and to establish a South Asian Cultural Center to promote the distinctive arts of South Asia. They requested the Government of Sri Lanka to circulate a concept paper on the issues to be addressed by the meeting including financing arrangements for the proposed institute.

Enhancing Political Cooperation

6. The Heads of State or Government reiterated their commitment to the promotion of mutual trust and understanding and, recognising that the aims of promoting peace, stability and amity and accelerated socio-economic cooperation may best be achieved by fostering good neighbourly relations, relieving tensions and building confidence, agreed that a process of informal political consultations would prove useful in this regard. The Heads of State or Government further recognized that this process would contribute to the appreciation of each other's problems and perceptions as well as for decisive action in agreed areas of regional cooperation.

Appraisal of SAARC Activities

7. The Heads of State or Government continued their review of the nature, extent, and effectiveness of the cooperative activities of SAARC. They considered the Report and Recommendations of the Group of Eminent Persons mandated by the Ninth Summit in Male' to undertake a comprehensive appraisal of SAARC and to develop an Agenda for 2000 and beyond. They expressed appreciation for the Chairman of the Ninth Summit, His Excellency Mr. Maumoon Abdul Gayoom, the President of the Maldives for convening the Group of Eminent Persons (GEP) and encouraging them to complete their work within the time frame given to them by the Ninth SAARC Summit.

8. The Heads of State or Government directed the Council of Ministers to examine the Report of the Group of Eminent Persons in depth at their next Session, taking into consideration the views of Member States with regard to the viability of the recommendations and the method of their implementation.

SAARC in the Changing International Economic Environment

9. The Heads of State or Government assessed the implications of current global economic developments on the economies of South Asia and other developing countries. They noted the profundity of the wide-spread changes being effected in the economic, technological, social and information

fields and their apparent unpredictability. They expressed serious concern over the severe distortions produced by the process of unrestrained globalisation as has been evidenced in the downturn of economies of several Asian States. The challenges and opportunities inherent in these fast evolving developments could best be met and the full potential of South Asia realized through effective practical regional and bilateral cooperation among Member States.

10. They noted that the benefits of the so described "liberalization" have been disappointingly asymmetrical with the process proceeding at a much slower pace in areas of special interest to developing countries. Increased opportunities in trade and investment have bypassed many developing countries. The Least Developed Countries have in particular been marginalised through a series of developments including the shrinking of ODA, concessional and other financial flows to these countries.

11. The Heads of State or Government noted the initiation of links between SAARC and economic unions and trading groups that were emerging in the wake of globalization and liberalization and considered how best relationships of mutual benefit could be established.

12. The Heads of State or Government observed that following the WTO Ministerial Conference in Geneva, a process has been initiated at the WTO where implementation issues, built in agenda issues, issues arising out of the WTO Ministerial Conference and other multi-lateral trade issues will be considered

with a view to making recommendations to the next Ministerial Conference of the WTO in 1999. These issues and the decisions arising from this process will have far-reaching consequences for our development strategies and prospects. The Heads of State or Government, therefore, resolved that SAARC countries would endeavour to coordinate their decisions on these issues in areas of common concern so as to protect and promote the interest of the developing countries. They expressed concern about the erection of protectionist barriers and the tendency to impose arbitrary "norms" relating to labour conditions, environmental regulations, governance and other extraneous issues to regulate trade exchanges, which would amount to additional non-tariff barriers, that would have the effect of restricting market access for developing countries including preferential access by Least Developed Countries (LDCs) into markets of developed countries. They agreed on the need for collective strategies to promote a rule-based, non-discriminatory and equitable international trading system in which the interests and concerns of developing countries would be fully safeguarded and served.

13. The Heads of State or Government noted that emerging issues relating to copyright, patents and marketing franchises including on foodgrains, plants and herbs indigenous to South Asia require firm collective responses to preserve these bio-resources from unregulated commercial exploitation by extra-regional interests. They emphasized in this regard, the principle of sustainable development of bio-resources and the provisions of the UN Convention

on Bio-diversity which provided for regulated access to such resources on terms and conditions to be agreed upon with the State in which such resources are located.

14. The Heads of State or Government cautioned that potential efforts to formulate a new Multilateral Investment Agreement should not overlook the need to ensure the continued independence of developing countries and Least Developed Countries (LDCs) to formulate specific investment policies appropriate to their stage of development.

15. While reviewing the beneficial effects of globalization, the Heads of State or Government stressed the fact that systemic crises are becoming unpredictable with increased globalization. They expressed their concern about the shortcomings of the international monetary and financial system, and its tardiness in anticipating impending financial market crises sufficiently in advance, so that pre-emptive remedial action be adopted. They noted that the problem is systemic, and not unique to Asia, nor confined to emerging economies, and that it can have global ramifications, unless more fundamental reforms are put in place.

16. They recognized the risk that ad-hoc approaches, however prompt, once crises supervene, may lead to excessive social costs in the attempt to restore financial discipline. More effective social safety nets would, therefore, need to be devised for protecting vulnerable groups and a more appropriate balance between financing and adjustment found in a reformed international system or architecture, if both the economic and social aspirations of SAARC

countries are to be realized. They acknowledged the need to strengthen the individual financial systems of SAARC countries through enhancing institutional capacity, surveillance mechanisms as well as through closer consultations on, and coordination of macro-economic policies where appropriate.

17. The Heads of State or Government recognized that notwithstanding all national and regional endeavours for economic development and financial stability, the pervasive global economic environment continued to exert a major, sometimes negative influence on the outcome of these endeavours.

18. Against this background of the need to address systemic issues, they agreed on the vital imperative for strengthened cooperation among SAARC Members to identify, analyze and effectively contend with the complex multi-faceted challenges inherent in the global economic environment that is changing so radically, particularly in this last decade preceding the new millennium. They acknowledged the need to enhance the collective capacity of SAARC in respect of policy analysis, with a specific emphasis on international financial, monetary, trade and investment issues and their domestic ramifications.

19. The Heads of State or Government also expressed their abhorrence over the practice of imposition of unilateral coercive economic measures as an instrument of policy against developing countries. They called for their immediate cessation.

20. They stressed the need for more efficient capacity building to enable informed decision-making in these areas to enable innovative collective intervention to

safeguard South Asian interests in international negotiations, as well as to develop some edge for effective leverage in such negotiations. The Heads of State or Government agreed on the urgent need for harnessing the rich intellectual and resource capacity of South Asia for this purpose.

21. The Heads of State or Government requested Sri Lanka, as Chairperson of the 10th Summit, to conduct consultations with Member States for the convening of a network of researchers comprising members of the Private Sector, Central Banks, Planning Ministries, Research Institutes and eminent economists nominated by Governments to identify, analyse and help SAARC faced up to current global, financial and economic developments affecting the region. They requested Sri Lanka to co-ordinate on necessary practical measures while keeping Member States informed in the matter. Heads of State or Government welcomed the offer of Sri Lanka to host a meeting in Colombo of representatives of SAARC, nominated by their Governments to study the matter further and report with practical recommendations on the matter in advance of the 21st Session of the Council of Ministers to facilitate early decisions.

Acceleration of Economic Cooperation

22. The Heads of State or Government assessed progress made in the two rounds of negotiations already undertaken under SAPTA. They decided that the third round should be concluded well before the Twenty-first Session of the Council of Ministers. The Heads of State or Government decided that to

accelerate progress in the next round of SAPTA negotiations, deeper preferential tariff concessions should be extended to products which are being actively traded, or are likely to be traded, among Members; that discriminatory practices and non-tariff barriers should be simultaneously removed on items in respect of which tariff concessions are granted or have been granted earlier. Measures to remove structural impediments should also be taken in order to move speedily towards the goal of SAFTA. They also directed that domestic content requirements under SAPTA Rules of Origin should be reduced and that the SAPTA Committee of Participants should meet by mid-October '98 in Colombo to finalise the extent of reduction in keeping with the decision of the Second SAARC Commerce Ministers' Meeting. The Heads of State or Government reaffirmed that measures to enable smaller and Least Developed Countries to benefit equitably from economic liberalization were specially important.

23. The Heads of State or Government reiterated the importance of achieving SAFTA as mandated by the Ninth SAARC Summit. To this end they decided that a Committee of Experts, in consultation with Member States, be constituted with specific Terms of Reference (TOR) to work on drafting a comprehensive treaty regime for creating a free trade area. The Heads of State or Government expressed the view that such a treaty must incorporate, among other things, binding time-frames for freeing trade, measures to facilitate trade, and provisions to ensure an equitable distribution of benefits of trade to all states, especially for smaller and least developed countries, including mechanisms for compensation of

revenue loss. They emphasised the importance of finalising the text of the regulatory framework by the year 2001.

24. The Heads of State or Government agreed that the benefits of economic liberalization would be more extensive and better balanced through the promotion of trade- creating joint ventures, investment and trade in services such as tourism.

25. The Heads of State or Government noted with satisfaction the outcome of the Second Meeting of the SAARC Commerce Ministers in Islamabad and welcomed their decision to coordinate SAARC's position on issues of common concern at the WTO. They welcomed in this connection the Declaration issued by the SAARC Commerce Ministers on the eve of the Second WTO Ministerial Meeting in Geneva, setting out a SAARC approach on these issues. Recognizing that critical issues would be decided at the Third WTO Ministerial Conference in the USA in 1999, the Heads of State or Government urged SAARC Commerce Ministers to work closely with a view to evolving better co-ordinated positions on all issues. They directed the Consultative Group of SAARC Permanent Representatives to the WTO at Geneva to consult closely with like-minded countries to advance the interests of developing countries at all WTO Conferences.

26. The Heads of State or Government noted the progress made in preparations for the Second SAARC Trade Fair to be held in Sri Lanka from September 8-15, 1998. The Heads of State or Government welcomed the offer of Bangladesh to host the Third Meeting of SAARC Commerce Ministers in 1999 and

the offer of Pakistan to stage the Third SAARC Trade Fair in 1999.

People to People Contact

27. The Heads of State or Government noted arrangements being finalized by Sri Lanka to host the First SAARC Film Festival in Colombo in 1998 in commemoration of the 50th Anniversary of the Independence of Sri Lanka.

28. The Heads of State or Government stressed that more convenient travel connections between SAARC countries were essential to facilitate fruitful interaction among people in the region, in particular, professional groups, creative artistes, pilgrims and journalists.

29. The Heads of State or Government considered means of encouraging more productive co-operation and collaboration between governments and the private sectors, including in the commissioning of studies relating to regional economic interaction.

30. They welcomed the contribution made by the SAARC Chamber of Commerce and Industry in facilitating the engagement of the private sector in regional economic interaction as well as initiating linkages with other regions for the purpose of promoting SAARC exports. The Heads of State or Government noted that a document entitled "Road Map to SAFTA" was presented by the President of the SAARC Chamber of Commerce and Industry (SCCI) to the Chairperson of the Twentieth Session of the Council of Ministers.

Links with Other International and Regional Organizations

31. The Heads of State or Government noted links initiated between SAARC and other international and regional organizations. They considered the prospects for the development of SAARC projects and programmes in association with such organizations with which SAARC has cooperative arrangements as well as through other forms of cooperation. The Heads of State or Government were of the view that priority needs to be given in establishing contact with those regional groupings which have experience in economic cooperation and functional regional cooperation.

32. The Heads of State or Government also noted proposals for developing cooperation between SAARC and individual States outside the region. They requested the Council of Ministers to consider such proposals with a view to developing such contacts on the basis of mutual benefit and for the advancement of SAARC objectives.

Projection of Commom Positions

33. The Heads of State or Government reiterated their resolve to promote the articulation of joint positions at the United Nations and other fora where such action would be in the clear interest of all members of the Association.

Sub-Regional Cooperation

34. With the objective of enhancing regional solidarity and promoting overall development within SAARC, the Heads of State or Government encouraged the development of specific projects relevant to the individual needs of three or more Member States under the provisions of Articles VII and X of the Charter.

Security of Small States

35. The Heads of State or Government recognized that due to their particular vulnerability, small States require special measures of support from the international community for the safeguarding of their sovereign independence and territorial integrity. They reiterated that real protection of small States should be firmly rooted in scrupulous adherence to the UN Charter, the rule of law and strict adherence to universally accepted principles and norms related to sovereign rights and territorial integrity of all States irrespective of size. This, they stressed should be ensured by all the countries either severally or collectively through the pursuit of appropriate action.

Special Measures for Least Developed and Land-Locked Countries

36. The Heads of State or Government emphasised the need for priority action on various international development commitments, such as the Paris Declaration and the Programme of Action for LDCs for the 1990s.

37. While noting with deep concern that economic growth in the Least Developed and Land-Locked Countries is not progressing well, the Heads of State or Government stressed the need to take special measures for accelerating the process of development. They emphasised the need to fulfil the internationally agreed aid targets for ensuring accelerated and sustained economic growth in developing countries particularly in the Least Developed Countries. They stressed on the need for adequate resources to facilitate implementation of economic reform programmes in SAARC countries.

38. The Heads of State or Government emphasised that the review of the criteria for the determination of LDC status for consideration by the United Nations General Assembly this year, must take into account the special significance of the extent and magnitude of incidence of poverty in the poorest countries and the special vulnerabilities of small island states.

Education and Literacy

39. The Heads of State or Government were in agreement that illiteracy was a major impediment to economic development and social emancipation and that the eradication of illiteracy in the Region including through co-operative endeavours within SAARC must continue to be pursued resolutely.

40. The Heads of State or Government noted that the concepts of Open Learning and Distance Education could help substantially towards equal opportunities and access to knowledge. The Heads of State or Government directed that SAARC should build on

the substantial expertise already existing in the Region in the field of open education, by establishing a SAARC Forum of Vice Chancellors of Open Universities. This Forum, consisting of regional leaders in the field, should strengthen cooperation in areas such as the sharing and joint development of programmes, credit transfers for specific programmes and the translation of existing programmes.

41. The Heads of State or Government urged the Forum, to spearhead the development of distance education outside the Open University System as well, drawing on the advances in Information Technology, to reach out to the remote and under-privileged sections. They welcomed the offer of Sri Lanka to host a meeting of Vice-Chancellors of SAARC Open Universities during the last quarter of 1998 to discuss the modalities for the establishment of the Forum and to draw up a programme to achieve the objectives identified by the Heads of State or Government. The Heads of State or Government requested the Forum to report to the Standing Committee on a continuous basis on its programmes.

Eradication of Poverty in South Asia

42. The Heads of State or Government reiterated the commitment of SAARC to the eradication of poverty in the Region at the earliest possible, preferably by the year 2002. They emphasised the need to encourage maximum participation by target groups in the formulation and implementation of poverty eradication programmes. The Heads of State or Government were of the view that such participation

is essential for success of efforts in this field. They stressed the need for effective utilisation of the SAARC Three-Tier Mechanism on Poverty Eradication and in that context welcomed the offer of the Government of Pakistan to host the next meeting of the SAARC Finance/Planning Ministers under the Mechanism in October 1998.

43. The Heads of State or Government noted that the South Asian countries have provided leadership in developing and implementing Micro Credit Programmes, which have immense potential to contribute to the eradication of poverty. They were of the view that their respective programmes in this regard have proven to be effective and Member States would benefit by sharing experiences and exchanging information and expertise in this important area.

44. The Heads of State or Government noted that Human Resource Development is a key element in any poverty eradication programme. The Heads of State or Government, therefore, agreed that once the SAARC Centre for Human Resource Development in Islamabad is established, it could look in to the possibility of its contributing to the strengthening of the human resource development components of the regional poverty eradication programmes.

Social Charter

45. The Heads of State or Government reviewed the progress made in the social sector by SAARC and determined that, in order to increase effectiveness, it would be necessary to develop, beyond national

plans of action, a regional dimension of action including a specific role for SAARC. In this context, they agreed that it would be necessary for SAARC to develop a Social Charter, which would focus on drawing up targets with a broad range to be achieved across the region in the areas of poverty eradication, population stabilisation, the empowerment of women, youth mobilisation, human resource development, the promotion of health and nutrition and the protection of children. The Heads of State or Government further directed the Council of Ministers to initiate work on drawing up a Social Charter.

Communications

46. The Heads of State or Government welcomed the results of the First Conference of SAARC Communication Ministers held in Colombo in May, 1998. They noted that technological advances were making telecommunications an important medium for socio-economic development and developing commercial and business relations as well as promotion of people-to-people contact. They called for the speedy implementation of the Plan of Action adopted by the First Meeting of the SAARC Communication Ministers.

Tourism

47. The Heads of State or Government recognized that further efforts were required for South Asia to effectively tap the economic potential afforded by the global tourist industry as well as to encourage intra-

SAARC tourism. They welcomed the convening of the First SAARC Tourism Ministers' Meeting in Colombo as a step towards this end and called for the effective implementation of its decisions, including the encouragement of active private sector participation in the promotion of tourism, both intra-regionally and internationally, simplification of visa-procedures for tourists and pilgrims, more convenient air and other travel links among SAARC countries including special regional fares and the co-ordination of activities of tour operators.

48. The Heads of State or Government identified the need to strengthen the existing air services between their respective Capitals, with a view to both facilitating tourism as well as people to people contacts. They called in this regard, for an early meeting of the Chairpersons/Chief Executive Officers of the national air lines.

Science and Technology

49. The Heads of State or Government noted that the development of a regional self-reliance capability for South Asia in scientific research and development was essential, given a global context in which barriers to the free flow of technology still remained in place. The Heads of State or Government appreciated the efforts to foster under the SAARC umbrella, collective co-operation in this field.

50. The Heads of State or Government welcomed the offer by the Government of India to hold a Special Meeting of SAARC Science and Technology Ministers to consider a SAARC Technology Initiative to

Identify and implement specific regional projects in rural areas which would have the direct impact in improving the day-to-day life of people there. Such an initiative could include rural telecommunications, drinking water and sanitation and improvement of life standards.

51. The Heads of State or Government reiterated their earlier call for the effective and rapid institutionalization of SAARC co-operation in the field of bio-technology. They pointed out that South Asia with its vast reservoir of bio-diversity and tropical climate, has substantial potential for bio-industry development on a sustainable basis. Many of the food and nutritional needs of the SAARC region could be met by the application of bio-technology. Contemporary developments in intellectual property and patent law, moreover, heightened the need for vigilance against encroachment on the regional bio-diversity heritage by external entities.

52. The Heads of State or Government accordingly requested the Standing Committee, with assistance of the SAARC Secretariat, to report to the forthcoming Twenty-First Session of the Council of Ministers on practical and cost effective measures towards rapidly operationalising SAARC cooperation in bio-technology.

Environment

53. The Heads of State or Government expressed their deep satisfaction at the positive outcome of the Environment Ministers' Conference held in Malé in

October 1997, and called for the effective and early implementation of the SAARC Environment Action Plan. In this context, they welcomed the offer of Maldives to prepare a feasibility study on the establishment of a Coastal Zone Management Centre. The Heads of State or Government also committed their governments to prepare National Environment Action Plans and State of the Environment Reports before the end of 1998.

54. The Heads of State or Government expressed their satisfaction over the adoption of a common position by Member States prior to the Third Session of the Conference of the Parties to the United Nations Framework Convention on Climate Change, held in Kyoto, Japan and welcomed the adoption of the Kyoto Protocol to the United Nations Framework Convention on Climate Change in December 1997, and underscored the importance of the Protocol for the protection of the climate system. They urged all industrial countries to ratify the Protocol and to undertake urgent and effective steps to implement the commitments undertaken by them to reduce their emissions of green-house gases.

55. The Heads of State or Government also emphasised the need for complementary action by organisations and institutions in the region in their efforts to protect the environment and achieve sustainable development in the region.

56. The Heads of State or Government noted that the SAARC Environment Ministers would be meeting in Sri Lanka in late 1998. They urged that the Ministers should at this forthcoming meeting also mandate any specific measures required for SAARC to further

strengthen cooperation on environment issues, with other international or regional organizations engaged in the same field.

Youth

57. The Heads of State or Government affirmed the importance they attached to providing adequate opportunities to youth in South Asia to participate productively in national development and underscored the need for developing programmes in this regard at the national and regional levels.

Children

58. Recalling targets and objectives set out in the Rawalpindi Declaration of 1996, the Heads of State or Government noted that the 1997 Review of the Situation of Children in South Asia had revealed progress in the reduction of infant mortality and increased coverage of immunization programmes. They stressed, however, that continued efforts required to be sustained in these areas. Serious efforts were also required in respect of education for all children and the reduction of gender disparities. In addition to national programmes, the Heads of State or Government called for the identification of practical regional programmes which could benefit from cooperation with relevant regional and international organisations with which SAARC has cooperative arrangements for the promotion of the welfare of children.

59. The Heads of State or Government condemned the exploitation of children by terrorist groups in hostilities and called for special measures for the psychological, physical and social rehabilitation of child victims. In this respect, the Heads of State or Government noted the initiative taken by Maldives in pursuance of their directive at the Ninth SAARC Summit in drafting the Convention on Regional Arrangements for the Promotion of Child Welfare in South Asia. They welcomed the offer of Maldives to hold an Expert Group Meeting to finalise the draft Convention for its adoption at the Eleventh SAARC Summit.

Situation of Women and The Girl Child

60. The Heads of State or Government noted that many groups of women and girl children in South Asia continue to be in disadvantaged positions and lack equal opportunities for economic and social development. They were of the view that sustained efforts and practical affirmative action was required to offset the effects of discriminatory, social and psychological perceptions and to empower women through affirmative action, including where necessary, legislative measures. The Heads of State or Government condemned in particular violence against women and acts of discrimination and humiliation which tend to depress the status of women. They also expressed concern over the plight of women and girl children in situations of conflict. Equal opportunities in education, health facilities and nutrition were vital for the integration of women in

the mainstream of national development. They agreed to work in close association, where possible, with professional and other women's groups in the region to ameliorate their conditions.

61. The Heads of State or Government recalled that the Ninth SAARC Summit expressed concern at the trafficking of women and children within and between countries and pledged to coordinate efforts of Member States to take effective measures to address this problem. In this context, they welcomed the finalisation of the draft text on the Regional Convention on Combating the Crime of Trafficking in Women and Children for Prostitution and noted that this would be a vital instrument in dealing with this problem. They approved that the Convention be signed at the Eleventh SAARC Summit.

62. The Heads of State or Government also recommended that the feasibility of establishing a Regional Fund for Rehabilitation of Victims of Trafficking in Women and Children for Prostitution on a voluntary basis may be explored.

63. The Heads of State or Government were also of the view that the scope of the Convention should be broadened to cover purposes other than prostitution.

64. The Heads of State or Government noted that a gender disaggregated data-base on the basis of data provided by Member States would be a valuable means of assisting the formulation of national and regional policies and programmes in respect of women and the girl child.

Health

65. The Heads of State or Government noted the rich heritage of traditional systems of medicine (TSM) in the region. They observed that regional cooperation in this area would be worthwhile and relevant for meeting basic health needs. They welcomed the offer of India to host the First Health Ministers Conference to evolve proposals for cooperation in this field.

66. The Heads of State or Government urged that the regional pharmaceutical industries should strengthen cooperation. They were further of the view that the Member States could establish Action Committees in terms of Article VII of the SAARC Charter for such cooperation, if required.

Disabled Persons

67. The Heads of State or Government recalled the Islamabad Resolution on Disabled Persons and underscored the importance of having a very definite humanistic approach to ensuring the welfare of the 100 million disabled persons of this region. In this respect, the Heads of State or Government accepted the proposal of the Prime Minister of Bangladesh for the establishment of a SAARC Voluntary Fund for Disabled Persons.

Information

68. The Heads of State or Government welcomed the recommendations of the First Meeting of SAARC Information Ministers held in Dhaka in April, 1998

and the offer of Pakistan to host the Second Meeting of Information Ministers of SAARC Countries.

69. The Heads of State or Government called for concerted endeavours for the promotion of practical programmes among South Asian countries, including through professional organizations, in the field of information and media exchanges benefitting from technological advances. Such action would help promote deeper understanding of issues common to the region, as well as to project a more balanced view of developments in the region. They welcomed the offer of India to host the First Meeting of SAARC Editors and Journalists.

Terrorism and Drug Trafficking

70. The Heads of State or Government recognized that the Member States and peoples of South Asia continue to face the serious threat of terrorism in all its forms and manifestations and drug trafficking. They reiterated their firm commitment to combat these activities in the region. They emphasized the urgent need to complete enabling legislation in order to implement the SAARC Regional Conventions on Suppression of Terrorism and on Narcotic Drugs and Psychotropic Substances.

71. The Heads of State or Government urged all Member States to enhance cooperation against terrorism, wherever, by whomever, against whoever it occurs and to fully observe and implement the SAARC Regional Convention on Terrorism.

72. The Heads of State or Government affirmed that criminal acts intended to provoke a state of terror in

the general public, a group of persons or particular persons, for whatever purposes, are unjustifiable in any circumstances.

73. The Heads of State or Government recalled the adoption of the 1996 UN Declaration on Measures to Eliminate International Terrorism and urged all Member States to work towards its implementation. They called for international action to prevent the abuse of Refugee Conventions and to halt activities which help terrorist groups to collect funds for their activities in South Asia.

74. The Heads of State or Government noted that two SAARC Conferences on Cooperation in Police Matters had been held since 1996. They called for the continued sharing of expertise with regard to the different areas of police investigation, and investigation of organized crime and drug related crimes.

Universal Declaration of Human Rights

75. The Heads of State or Government taking note of the 50th Anniversary of the Universal Declaration of Human Rights, reaffirmed their commitment to the further promotion of human rights and fundamental freedoms by strengthening the respective national institutions in South Asia in this field. The Leaders agreed that tolerance and mutual accommodation, combined with the strengthening of participatory governance, constituted the foundation for the sustainable economic and social development of the SAARC region.

International Political Developments

76. The Heads of State or Government consulted informally on a range of international issues, particularly those which have a bearing on South Asia. They re-affirmed their strong commitment to the purposes and principles of the UN Charter and agreed that their delegations would work closely in the ongoing negotiations for the reform and strengthening of the UN system, so that the Organisation could be more democratic, efficient and financially viable and responsive to the interests of its membership, especially developing countries.

77. The Heads of State or Government also underscored the importance of the role of the Non-Aligned Movement in promoting a just and equitable global order and called for the further enhancing of the efforts of the Movement to influence positively contemporary international relations. In this context, they expressed full confidence that the Twelfth Summit of the Movement scheduled to take place in South Africa would contribute towards augmenting the Movement's effectiveness.

78. The Heads of State or Government were of the view that stability, peace and security in South Asia could not be considered in isolation of the global security environment. Although great power rivalry which the NAM had consistently opposed, no longer posed a serious threat and the danger of a global nuclear conflagration had abated, yet some States had sought to maintain huge arsenals of nuclear weapons. The NPT and the CTBT, to which some SAARC members were signatories, had not led to any progress towards nuclear disarmament nor prevented proliferation.

They underscored their commitment to the complete elimination of nuclear weapons and the need for promoting nuclear disarmament on a universal basis, under effective international control. They recognised that global non-proliferation goals cannot be achieved in the absence of progress towards nuclear disarmament and in this context called upon all nuclear weapon states, whether party or non-party to the NPT to engage constructively through a transparent and credible process of negotiations at the Conference on Disarmament.

79. The Heads of State or Government therefore urged the Conference on Disarmament to commence negotiations on a comprehensive, universal and non-discriminatory international instrument prohibiting the use or the threat of nuclear weapons as well as eliminating such weapons in existing arsenals.

80. The Heads of State or Government noted the outcome of the recent UN Diplomatic Conference on the establishment of an International Criminal Court and the fact that the Conference had not addressed such issues as the crime of drug trafficking and the crime of terrorism with its use of indiscriminate violence aimed at innocent civilians and use of weapons of mass destruction. They emphasised the need to ensure that the proposed Court should respect the sovereignty of States consistent with the principle of complementarity with national jurisdiction on which the Statute of the Court is based.

81. The Heads of State or Government welcomed the enhanced status accorded to Palestine at UN fora. They however expressed growing concern at

numerous setbacks affecting the peace process in the Middle East, including illegal attempts to change the jurisdiction and borders of Jerusalem. They re-affirmed their support for the achievement of a just, lasting and comprehensive peace based on Security Council Resolution 242 (1967) and Resolution 338 (1973) to restore the inalienable national rights of the Palestinian people.

82. The Heads of State or Government called for intensification of efforts for promoting peace and stability at the global and regional levels for realising universal progress and prosperity.

Dates and Venue of the Eleventh Meeting of the Heads of State or Government

83. The Heads of State or Government accepted with deep appreciation the offer of His Majesty's Government of Nepal to host the Eleventh SAARC Summit in the second half of 1999.

84. The Heads of State or Government of Bangladesh, Bhutan, India, the Maldives, Nepal and Pakistan expressed their appreciation for the skilful manner in which the President of the Democratic Socialist Republic of Sri Lanka had conducted the meeting and guided its deliberations, in her capacity as Chairperson. They also expressed their deep gratitude for the warm and generous hospitality extended to them by the Government and the people of Sri Lanka and the excellent arrangements made for the Summit and the meetings preceding it.